Cara M —

Eccomi qua!

Amore

R.

RENATA TEBALDI

The Woman and the Diva

RENATA TEBALDI

The Woman and the Diva

-- VICTOR SEROFF --

Appleton-Century-Crofts, Inc.
New York

To my dear Nana

-- *Illustrations* --

vii

FOLLOWING PAGE 150

RENATA TEBALDI

The Woman and the Diva

-- *Chapter 1* --

"*Mamma, Mamma . . .*"—"*Renata, Renata . . .*"

The two women fell into each other's arms weeping.
But their tears were not caused by sorrow. Mamma Tebaldi had been praying all morning, awaiting Renata's
return. They were living at 13 Via Broggi in Milan, where
two days before they had come to stay temporarily because Renata had an important appointment—the most
important of her young life. They had rented one room
with the right to use the kitchen in Signora Clara Poccinesta's small apartment. Although, with the superstition

1

of the stage, Renata did not talk about the reason for their sudden arrival in Milan, the old landlady must have whispered about it to her neighbors, for it seemed as if the whole little house was awaiting the result in tense and silent excitement. And indeed, as Renata rushed upstairs, taking two steps at a time, she noticed several doors in the corridor slowly opening and curious eyes following her. But Renata could think of nothing but her mother.

"It was the happiest moment of my life," Renata Tebaldi told me, reminiscing about it many years later. "I was so excited when I burst into the room that I almost lifted Mamma right off her feet."

Renata actually whirled her mother twice around the room before she could tell her what had happened. Even today, when speaking about it, Renata stops for a moment, as if she were collecting herself before singing one of her favorite arias.

"I had run as fast as I could all the way home from La Scala. It seemed to me that morning that the tramcars were unusually slow and I was too impatient, I couldn't wait to tell everything to Mamma. But even before I could say anything, Mamma knew that everything had gone well. All I could do was to keep nodding and swallow the tears—we kissed and cried."

Renata had just returned from her audition with Arturo Toscanini. This was in May of 1946 and she was then twenty-four years old. During the past two weeks she had been singing at the opera house in Brescia. One day, while they were rehearsing Pietro Mascagni's *L'Amico Fritz,* one of her colleagues, Giacinto Prandelli, the tenor, was called to come to Milan for an audition with Toscanini. Every musician in Italy knew that the Maestro had at last returned to Milan after an absence of almost seven years. They had all heard that he wished to select the most talented young singers for the gala concert with which he planned to "reinaugurate" the famous opera house of Milan, La Scala, rebuilt after it had been damaged during the war. Renata, like the others in the cast, looked with envy at the lucky tenor as he left the theater in Brescia to prepare for his journey.

"A few days later Prandelli returned," Renata continued her story, "and when I saw him again he told me that while he was waiting his turn he had seen the list of those whom the Maestro had chosen to audition and that my name was on it. I practically lost my head. I did not want to sing any more at Brescia. Somehow these five performances of *L'Amico Fritz* seemed to me 'too local' to lead to anything important. I could think of only one thing—the coming audition with the Maestro. Everything else ceased to matter. I was beside myself. I did not know what to do. Everyone advised me to be calm and just wait for the call. That was all very easy to say, but I don't remember how many days and nights I lived through in utter agony.

"Finally one day I received a telephone call from Luigi

3

Oldeni—he was then the secretary in the administration at La Scala. I was too excited to understand a single word he said, except that my audition was to be on Saturday at ten o'clock in the morning. Now I no longer remember the date—it may have been May 10. Please don't ask me what I did then. I don't even remember whether I put down the receiver. I was at rehearsal in the opera house but I never gave it a thought, just ran home to tell Mamma."

Next day mother and daughter went to Milan and on the appointed Saturday Renata got up very early to give herself enough time to prepare for the momentous event. She dressed carefully, but soon discovered that there was not much else she could do. She had few clothes to choose from; she had only one coat "for any hour of the day or night," as she says now, and at that time she wore no makeup, except for a slight touch of lipstick. Her dark chestnut hair was long and fell in waves to her shoulders. On the whole she looked like a healthy country girl who felt there was no sense in sitting very long in front of the mirror. Her mother carefully examined Renata's simple two-piece blue dress and nodded with approval. Renata wore no jewelry except for a small gold wrist watch. She did a little "vocalizing"—she was too nervous to do much —prayed once more, kissed her mother and left the house.

It was still far too early for her appointment and she decided to walk to La Scala. On the way she stopped at a newspaper stand and bought *Domenica del Corriere,* an illustrated paper. This, she said, she did to give herself courage, more self-assurance, and perhaps even an air of nonchalance. She walked into La Scala at nine-thirty, still half an hour too early, but she was too nervous to remain on the street. She entered a small room and sat there waiting, turning the pages of her newspaper, trying to interest herself in the pictures, but for all the impression they made she might have been holding it upside down.

On the dot of ten o'clock the door opened and an usher walked into the room.

"Which of you is Renato Tebaldi?" he asked, using the masculine form of her first name.

For an instant Renata's heart sank. It flashed through her mind that perhaps it was all a mistake—they had been expecting a man. Hardly able to pronounce the words she asked if indeed there was a misunderstanding. "My name is Renata," she explained. But except for saying "Oh?" the usher paid no attention to her confusion. "Please come with me, Maestro Toscanini wishes to see you."

There are several large rooms at La Scala in addition to the auditorium, and among them two are well known, the Yellow Room, where rehearsals are often held, and the Red Room, which is also sometimes used for auditions. As Renata was ushered into the Red Room she crossed herself. Her knees almost gave way when she lifted her head and looked around.

"It was a very impressive room, all in red and gold with a large chandelier hanging from the ceiling and a very long table," Renata told me. "There sat the Maestro. He was looking at a paper in front of him on the table and I could not see his face, but I saw the two men who sat beside him. Later I learned who they were: one was the Maestro's son Walter, and the other Antonio Ghiringhelli, the director of La Scala."

As it happens, the Red Room (which is no longer red since four or five years ago it was completely redecorated) is not large at all. But at the time everything seemed "impressive" to Renata, and since I do not believe she ever saw the room again, she still feels that it and everything in it was of magnificent proportions.

After consulting his notes, Toscanini looked at her. "You are Signorina Tebaldi?" he asked.

"Yes, Maestro," Renata managed to murmur.

"Where do you come from?"

"I was born in Pesaro, but I am really *Parmigiana* [from Parma] . . . like you. . . ."

Toscanini looked startled. He may have been surprised at the somewhat impertinent way she said "like you," but Renata believes that his interest in her was aroused there and then because she had remembered that Parma was Toscanini's birthplace.

He put his arms on the table and, leaning over it, questioned her about her studies. When Renata mentioned the name of Carmen Melis, Toscanini looked pleased. He had always been a great admirer of her teacher and knew her very well.

"Well then, what are you going to sing for me?" he asked.

" 'La Mamma morta' from *Andrea Chenier*," Renata said firmly.

"Hm," Toscanini said, for this aria is known to be a difficult one.

"With whom did you study it?"

"With Signora Melis." Renata repeated the name of her teacher.

"Well then, go ahead," Toscanini said and nodded to the accompanist.

Today as then, Renata Tebaldi is a sensitive person. In everyday life, whenever she finds herself confronted with people she becomes shy, but the minute she is on the stage, the minute she begins to perform, this embarrassing feeling leaves her. Consequently, as she remembers it, as soon as she started to sing she forgot that Toscanini and the two other strange men were there listening to her. She even forgot that this was perhaps the most important moment in her life—she thought only of the music she was singing.

Toscanini listened carefully and then asked her to come back to the table. He wanted to talk to her. He wanted to know what else she could sing. "Desdemona in *Otello*," Renata said.

Again Toscanini looked surprised. But when in her

7

turn Renata asked what particular aria he would like to hear, he said, "The whole role, from beginning to end. Have you the score with you?" Renata did. She had come to the audition well armed, with the scores of several operas she might have the opportunity to sing for him. Actually he made her go through the last act only. At first, when she started to sing, she noticed that Toscanini was conducting, or perhaps it would be better to say marking the tempo, with his forefinger close to his face. Renata could see that apparently he did not like the tempi the accompanist was taking, and she began to follow him. Gradually, as she went on singing, Toscanini was conducting with his full arm and Renata followed him. He was particularly pleased, she could tell, with the "Ave Maria."

"Bravo, bravo," Toscanini finally said to her, and as she was leaving, he told his son Walter to write down her address.

Recently I spoke with Walter Toscanini about this audition and asked him whether, after Renata left the room, his father had said anything to him or Ghiringhelli about her singing. "No," Walter Toscanini said, "he only told me to write down her address. But there was nothing extraordinary about this. You see, only a few people realize that it was characteristic of my father never to praise anyone in superlative terms. My father expected a singer to be good; if he weren't he would criticize him, then he would have something to say, but otherwise he

8

actually found nothing unusual if one did his best. He was the same way with me as he was with his other children. If I ever said or did something intelligent it did not surprise him. However, it is true that he complimented Renata by saying 'Bravo,' but that was no more than to have said in English 'Good,' and that is as far as he would go."

By chance, I met Renata a few months later. I happened to be in Milan on a postwar cultural scouting mission for *Town & Country*, seeking to find out who in the field of music had survived and what new talent had been discovered of which we, during the war, had heard nothing. The rehabilitation of the bombed areas in Milan had hardly begun, but plans to repair the damage to La Scala were already complete and some of the work was actually in progress. As in the old days, the men connected with La Scala would gather at the little tables in the Galleria to discuss their professional and personal business and, of course, to gossip. When I joined one of these groups I was eagerly asked who in New York was popular among singers who had come from Italy. I mentioned Ezio Pinza, Ferruccio Tagliavini, and Licia Albanese. "Ah," they said, "wait till you hear one of our young singers. When she comes to New York she'll be a sensation. And," said the man raising his forefinger, while the others beamed with approval, "she is the most beautiful girl we have had on the stage for a long time."

Next day at the appointed hour Renata came to talk to

9

me at the same café. Indeed she was beautiful. She radiated so much grace and charm that I could see how everyone, including Toscanini, would be impressed. She was tall and carried herself straight and with a certain dignity, but it was her great blue eyes that arrested one's attention. That day she wore a simple dark summer dress and a large black straw hat. As she sat down at the table I think she soon became conscious that I was studying her face—her nose a little turned up, the beautifully drawn mouth, the two dimples in her cheeks and a row of beautiful white teeth.

Renata was timid and obviously not used to being interviewed, especially by foreigners. I spared her the ordeal of questioning and we chatted for a while about her career, which at that time was only in its embryo. She never mentioned her audition with Toscanini and was very modest about her accomplishments.

I remembered that she refused to have an ice cream because it was too dangerous for her voice, she said. Today she enjoys ice cream, but only when her singing dates are not imminent. She left with me the impression of a very serious young girl dedicated to her art, although she did say that she was engaged. Somehow it sounded as if this were of secondary importance. It was easy to predict that if her voice was as good as everyone claimed, she would go a long way on the lyric stage. Otherwise, at least it was clear she would make the lucky man to whom she was then engaged extremely happy.

10

Since that meeting I have watched her career both from afar and at close range. I have seen her suddenly change, at the age of thirty, from a girl into a young woman. But not until she agreed to let me write her life story did I really learn to know her more intimately. Perhaps she is joking, but now she even says that I know more about her than anyone in the world.

-- *Chapter 2* --

Although Renata has always claimed that she had a happy childhood, she has arrived at this conclusion, I imagine, because of her deeply religious nature and because she has resigned herself to accept life as it comes. Actually it was far from happy.

She was born on February 1, 1922, at five in the afternoon, in Pesaro, a small town on the Adriatic coast. She was a large baby, weighing ten pounds. Her mother used to tell her that it was one of the coldest days in her memory—everything was frozen. Was her mother speaking of the weather, or perhaps of the feeling in her own heart? For Renata's birth came at the time of a serious matrimonial crisis between her parents.

Her father, Teobaldi Tebaldi, a native of Pesaro, was about seven years younger than her mother, and was then twenty-six. As a boy he had studied cello at the Gioacchino Rossini Conservatory in Pesaro, but World War I put an end to his studies and his musical career. He was drafted into the army and because he was over six feet tall was posted to a regiment of grenadiers. During the battle on Monte Carso, in the Trentino, he was wounded in the leg, and it was while he was convalescing in an army hospital in Langhirano, near Parma, that he met Giuseppina Barbieri, Renata's mother, who worked there as a nurse. Giuseppina was born in Langhirano. "Like all the Barbieris," Renata explained to me. "For generations, they have been natives of Langhirano."

Giuseppina and Teobaldi were married in 1920 in Langhirano, but they soon settled down in a small apartment in Pesaro, where the Tebaldi family was living. At that time Teobaldi returned to his former occupation. As a cellist he played in the orchestras of provincial opera houses in such places as Bari, Rimini, Riccione and Ancona. At first the young couple seem to have been happy, but by the time Renata was born the romance apparently had cooled, and three months later Giuseppina took her newborn child back home to Langhirano and left her husband, who continued to live his own life in Pesaro.

13

Some people, claiming to know more than others, have suggested that Teobaldi was very much disappointed in having a daughter and not a son, and that on the whole the inhabitants of Pesaro were rather happy to see Giuseppina leave town—two females less to feed in a community which needed men. This sort of gossip does create a picture resembling one of Victor de Sica's films, where on a cold wintry day a mother dressed in an old worn-out overcoat, clutching in her arms her newborn baby, and dragging an old suitcase, slinks off to the station, while the shopkeepers and a few working women view her departure with a rather pleased air. Such an attitude is not uncommon in small towns in Italy.

But Renata never heard of this version. She told me that for a long time her mother did not explain what had really happened nor what was the true cause of her break with her husband. Renata suspected, however, and eventually Giuseppina admitted that it must have been her fault—she was a very jealous woman. Her husband was a handsome man, younger than she was, and she loved him very much. Teobaldi knew that he was handsome and that women liked him, and apparently Giuseppina's love was not sufficient for him. "He was not very attentive to Mamma," Renata tried delicately to explain to me. But all this Renata learned much later. As a child she knew nothing about it. She was simply told that her father had died.

Recently Renata showed me the place where she had

spent her childhood and adolescence. We drove from Milan to Parma, and then out on a country road for some ten miles to Langhirano. The country is flat, mostly uncultivated fields, and there is nothing interesting to see, except perhaps the old Castello Torrechiara on a nearby hill, from which Napoleon, so they say, carried away as "military booty" a great many treasures. It has been carefully preserved although there is nothing to see inside now except the bare walls. Yet the building is apparently considered a valuable and historic relic, which shows the comparative poverty of the countryside.

Langhirano is a small village and you can see it all in less than an hour. A Piazza Garibaldi is the center of it. It is not square, but irregular, almost oval, like so many squares in the Italian villages. Of the ten cafés in Langhirano three are on the square, and since the *piazza* is small, one can easily, I imagine, converse with friends sitting at the other cafés without leaving one's own table.

Giuseppina's father Luciano Barbieri was the postmaster there. The post office has only two windows, but it is an extremely busy one, not because the three thousand townspeople are such avid correspondents, but because a famous *prosciutto* and salami industry is centered in Langhirano. In fact the natives like to refer to their little village as the "capital of *prosciutto*."

Luciano Barbieri owned a large three-story house: the post office is located on the ground floor and the two apartments on the floors above were occupied by his

15

family. Besides this he owned a small store on the other side of the square, where he sold a little bit of everything —all sorts of commodities such as soap, oil, sausage, fruit, sweets, vegetables and household articles.

Next to the post office is a café where Renata insists they make the best ice cream in the world, and a few steps further on, a tower with a clock, which strikes every hour. Renata can still remember the sound of it as it sent her to school. Then she would run down a crooked street, wide enough for but one car, and pass the church where she sang as a child in the choir and a few stores with men's clothes and women's dresses hanging on the racks outside.

The Langhirano school is in a drab brown brick two-story building. The classrooms are just as drab: fifteen benches, each for two students, a teacher's desk on a small platform, and four walls, bare except for two holy pictures, a large cross and an old map of Europe. Here Renata spent the first four years of her schooling, until she was moved to the second floor into a similar classroom for another four years of her formal education.

On one side the school faces the Torrente di Parma, a river usually dry during the summer months. If you walk toward the park, consisting of a few not too healthy-looking trees and a couple of benches, you pass several *prosciutto* factories and an old cinema, where Renata saw *Ben Hur* in its original version three times. And that is all there is to Langhirano.

16

Nor does it have a pleasant climate. It lies in a valley and the hills are too far away to protect it from the wind. It is very cold in the winter and hot in the summer. But it is a quiet place; the inhabitants of Langhirano lead a very sedate life. They work, raise their children, sip *espressos* in the coffee-houses while playing cards or discussing local events and by ten in the evening they are in bed. The only difference in their summer schedule is that that they may stay up a bit later gossiping.

The Barbieris were a typical Langhirano family, only instead of gossiping in cafés they preferred to spend their evenings at home. Renata's grandmother Clotilde, also born Barbieri, kept house for the family. Sometimes, while she and her two daughters Giuseppina and Marianna were busy with the housework, or mending or sewing clothes, the younger generation—Renata with her two cousins, Clotilde, or Tilde, three years older, and Luciano, who was Renata's age—would join their father, Renata's uncle Valentino, in a lively game of lotto. Their grandfather usually remained in the adjoining room at his desk, writing.

Renata does not know what he was writing, but her aunt Marianna told me that he kept a diary, wrote many articles on economics and even a book about one of Garibaldi's men, which was published. He was an ardent Socialist, she said.

"My grandfather was a tall man with a severe expression in his eyes. He wore a beard and was very elegant."

(I have noticed that in describing men Renata likes to use the word "elegant." She refers to their clothes rather than to their manners.)

"He was also very musical. He used to play on an old and very much out-of-tune grand piano, and even compose all kinds of waltzes and mazurkas, with which he entertained us and his friends." These were never written down, but Renata's piano teacher sang for me at least one of the melodies, which she still remembers after some twenty-five years.

I have met some of Renata's relatives. When Tilde heard about our coming to Langhirano she arranged a luncheon party. Tilde is a good-looking woman. As one might expect of an Italian she has black hair and black eyes, but considering the fact that she lives in a country where people do not watch their diet, she is not fat. She works at the post office, and is married to Dante, also a Barbieri, who is a few years her senior. Dante is a jovial fellow who loves good food and good wine and laughs at the Americans who eat only sandwiches for lunch. He is an accountant in one of the municipal offices. These Barbieris are nice, simple people, extremely hospitable and not overburdened with problems and complexes.

At the same time I met Marianna, who must now be in her seventies, a frail little woman bent by age and suffering from rheumatism. She occupies the apartment on the top floor, where formerly Renata used to live with her mother. She joined us for lunch and although Renata told

18

me that she does not speak English I had the feeling that she understood a great deal—she is very inquisitive and listens intently to every word in a conversation. Marianna always lived with the family, except when she became occasionally "temperamental," according to Renata, and then she would go to Parma to work there at the post office. "So you see," Renata laughed, "the Barbieris sooner or later always land in a post office. My uncle Valentino also at one time worked in the post office. It is a tradition. And I too—if I did not have a voice—most probably I would be working at the post office," Renata concluded. She illustrated with her fist on the table how she would have been stamping envelopes.

-- Chapter 3 --

Renata was not a strong child. When she was three years old she was stricken with polio, which affected her legs. Her mother took her to a doctor in Parma, and later, every year Renata was taken to Salsomaggiore for a two-months cure. Giuseppina did not have any income—she had not taken a job when she returned home, but took care of the small store which belonged to her father. It would have been hard for her to meet the expenses involved in her daughter's illness if Valentino had not lived at that time in Parma, where he was a postmaster. They

20

stayed with him. Eventually Renata was cured, but even today she still feels a few reminders of the illness which affected her right hip.

Although this creates certain problems for her, Renata never speaks of it. Not only are her audiences completely unaware of the fact that she has made her brilliant career despite this handicap, but even most of the colleagues who perform with her know nothing about it. In fact, she is famous for her graceful walk in such roles as Floria Tosca.

She also suffered from frequent bouts of bronchitis, laryngitis and swollen glands in her throat—none of these maladies too good for a future singer. Being ill so much of the time had made her a rather irritable child, but apparently her grandparents always spoiled her. Renata's grandfather in many ways replaced her own father, and she loved her grandmother as much as she loved Giuseppina. When she misbehaved and her mother was going to spank her, she would run for protection to her grandmother and hide in her wide skirts.

"My happiest childhood memory is connected with a doll which Mamma gave me for Christmas," Renata once told me. "I was then about three or four years old. The doll's name was Marie-José, like that of the Belgian Princess who had married our Crown Prince," Renata explained. "She was about two feet high with blonde curls and blue eyes." Renata, who has blue eyes, of course thought she looked like the doll. She loved it. But one day she forgot it on the terrace of their home and the rain completely ruined Marie-José. Later, her mother bought her another doll, but Renata never cared for it.

I told Renata that it reminded me of a story about a little lamb who was thrown into a lion's cage. To everybody's surprise the lion did not devour the lamb and the two became good friends. Later, the little lamb fell sick and died. The lion was inconsolable, but when another lamb was put into his cage he paid no attention to him. Renata liked the story. "No," she said, "substitutes are never the right thing," and she gave me a look as if to suggest to me that she had just let me in on one of the important aspects of her character.

It seems to me that to this day Renata really loves dolls. She has quite a collection of them. Some of these dolls have been given her for good luck, and being, like most artists, very superstitious, she carries them to every performance and carefully arranges them in her dressing room.

Like most middle-class Italian children Renata went to a sort of kindergarten and then at the age of six entered an elementary school—coeducational, boys and girls. By then she had outgrown her capriciousness and became a good student. She was, however, not equally proficient in all subjects. She was not as good in arithmetic as she was in history and she liked best of all Italian composition and literature. Because of the polio she was denied all sports and strenuous games, and this may be one of the reasons why she had more friends among girls than boys.

She often stayed at home alone, she remembers, either reading or playing a game of her own invention. She would play "school" by placing in her room a row of chairs in a semicircle. These were her pupils. Then she would stand behind a small table, which served as the teacher's desk, and with a stick in her hand she would "lecture" them. She gave them marks, admonished and punished them.

At other times her friends would come to the house and then, supervised by Giuseppina, they would do their homework, or try to learn to do the needlework for which her mother was well known and admired. Renata also learned to ride a bicycle and her occupations and pleasures outside of school varied, except for one thing: she never missed going to a little bakery next to their house where she would feast every day on *pasta rosa,* small rectangular cakes made of almond paste, finely cut sugar and small *bonbons glacés.* Then with a completely satisfied air she would haughtily refuse to pay, charging them to her grandfather. She thought then that this Langhirano specialty was heavenly, and I think she still does. "Wait until you taste them," she said to me and her eyes sparkled. Before we left Langhirano she insisted that I should take a whole package of them with me.

Renata always had a sweet tooth, but now she says

with chagrin she cannot indulge it because she has to watch her weight. As a matter of fact Renata loves food —not fancy delicacies such as caviar, but plain wholesome food: spaghetti, lasagna and all kinds of Italian *pasta*. Unfortunately, for the same reason, she can only occasionally allow herself such pleasures, and when she does, she eats with such gusto that there cannot be any doubt of the sacrifices she has been making for the sake of her art.

During the winter her life in Langhirano was not particularly pleasant. It gets very cold there, as I have mentioned before—for the Italians, that is. The temperature drops below the freezing point. It begins to snow in November and the snow remains on the ground sometimes until April. Not being able to enjoy any form of sports, not even tobogganing, Renata did not have much fun. Although she has told me many times that her family was not poor, that they had everything they wanted, I am inclined to believe that it was not as comfortable as she imagines. Their apartment was cold; only one room, the sitting room, was heated, the rest of the place remained cold, and particularly the bedroom which she shared with her mother. Often, if she would leave a glass of water by the open window, on the following day she would find it frozen. To keep warm at night they used the old-fashioned method of placing hot bricks in their beds, only it was a *scaldaletto*—an Italian bed-warming contraption

—and during the day they wore warm clothes mostly made of cotton and wool. They could not afford furs. Consequently Renata suffered from frostbitten legs and feet and every winter had to use cod-liver oil both internally and externally. It seemed to help her.

Nevertheless Renata, like all little girls, did have some childhood pleasures, particularly during the holidays: Santa Lucia on December 13, Christmas, and St. Nicholas on January 6. In her memory all these festivities are connected with the special delicacies on which the Tebaldis feasted. Her mouth waters when she describes all the dishes, all the sweet cakes she then enjoyed. Listening to her you can almost taste the *tortellini capeletti,* filled with a mincemeat of pork and veal and cheese. They were prepared by Giuseppina, always an expert cook. Watching her mother Renata also learned to cook, but she says she is not particularly good at it, and frankly she is rather glad that she is not. Giuseppina always said that Renata was a better singer than a cook.

Among many Christmases which Renata remembers one stands apart in her memory, and for a good reason. It is a custom in Italy for children to put a letter under their father's plate at the Christmas table. Promising to be good, to study well and to be obedient, the child usually asks him to fulfill a Christmas wish. Whenever the other children would talk about this, happily anticipating the coming holidays, Renata felt more than ever that she did not have a father. She was ten years old and for some time had begun to wonder about her family relationships, but she kept the questions which bothered her to herself.

One day one of her schoolmates was discussing the letter she was planning to write to her father for Christmas. Renata kept silent. Suddenly the girl asked her, "And what will you ask for?"

"I cannot, my father is dead," Renata answered quietly.

"Your father is not dead," the girl said. "That is not true. I know it. I have heard my parents speak about him. He lives in Pesaro."

This was a far greater shock to her than when she first was told that he was dead, Renata has told me. "It was hard for me to see the other children's fathers come to fetch them at the school, sometimes play with them, bring them presents, but I got used to it, but then . . . I could not believe it. I could not believe he was alive. I ran to our schoolmistress and asked her about it."

The schoolmistress tried to calm her, sent her back to her class, and meanwhile telephoned to Giuseppina and related what had happened. Renata was excused from school and went home. There her mother tried to explain it all as best she could.

"Mamma was not prepared to tell me about it. She had hoped she would not have to until I was older, and anyway I was much too young to follow the story. All I knew was that my father was alive, and if I would write him perhaps I could see him."

Teobaldi promptly answered her letter, spoke of his love for her and his desire to see her. Thereupon Giuseppina and Valentino held a long conference. Finally it was decided to let him come to see his child. A few days later he arrived. No one met him at the station. When he came to the house he talked for a long time with Valentino, then with Giuseppina. Renata was kept in her room until her mother came to fetch her.

"This is your daughter Renata, and this, Renata, is your father," she said as she brought Renata into the room.

"It took me a long time to learn to use the word 'Papa,'" Renata confided, "and even to get used to the idea that I had a father like all the other children. I was shy and perhaps even a bit frightened. I had never known what it meant to be caressed, to be patted or kissed by a father."

Teobaldi remained with them for twenty-five days. This voided the legal separation which Giuseppina had obtained after she had left him ten years before. Then he went back to Pesaro to arrange his affairs there. It was decided that he should no longer work as a cellist, but at first would help Giuseppina in the store and later take a job with a labor union which was offered to him.

He had not been gone more than a week when Giuseppina fell ill. She had to have a mastoid operation and the doctor was quite frank in telling her of the seriousness of her condition. He advised her at once to enter a hospital in Parma. This unexpected complication disturbed Giuseppina particularly because it happened just at the time when, after the reconciliation with Teobaldi, she was hoping to resume a happy life with her husband. She wrote to Teobaldi and asked him to return immediately so that he could stay with Renata while she was in Parma. Later, with her father, Renata visited Giuseppina in the hospital, but they were at home in Langhirano when the operation took place.

"She went in a *bella donna*," Renata said. "She came out disfigured. I cursed the surgeon—I wanted to kill him." It seems that during the operation by some accident the lights in the room went out and the surgeon, who was in the midst of his work, cut through a nerve which paralyzed one side of Giuseppina's face and deprived her of the hearing of one ear.

"It was one of the most dreadful things that happened to me in my childhood. My Mamma, my beautiful Mamma. . . ." Renata paused for a moment as she looked away. "But Mamma had a strong character. She did not complain, neither then nor when she returned home. She accepted it as her fate, as she taught me to accept everything in life." Thus Renata concluded her sad story.

The return of her father changed many things for Renata. Although life was not the way she used to imagine it would be, eventually it did, as she said, become more complete. But during the first three or four months she was very jealous of Teobaldi. Suddenly Giuseppina, who until then had centered her love exclusively on her daughter, became preoccupied with her husband. At times Renata even thought that her mother had lost all interest in her. Often her parents would sit together the whole evening discussing something, and Renata was not allowed to join them. Eventually, however, she sensed that her mother felt much happier and that her father loved them both.

His expression of love for Renata was not like that of her mother, it was not as tender; but he was attentive to her, brought her presents, never spanked her as her mother did quite often. In all the time Renata knew him he never raised his hand against her.

"I think," Renata once told me, "that it was his nature. He was rather cold and not at all affectionate. Perhaps this was also one of the reasons why my love for him could never have been equal to what I felt for my mother."

Today, looking back at her family relationships, Renata has definite ideas about marriage and divorce when children are involved. Her own case certainly proved to her how damaging it is for a child to grow up in a strained atmosphere. Renata is very religious and yet she cannot go along with the Italian law which does not permit divorce. On one hand she thinks that parents should remain together for the sake of a child, and on the other hand she does not see how two people can possibly continue to live together if they no longer love each other, and may even love someone else.

Generally speaking Renata is against the prohibition of divorce. "Why," she asks, "should a woman remain attached to a man if, for instance, he has committed a crime and has been sent to prison or if his behavior is incompatible with maintaining a respectable home and an honorable reputation for his wife?" But she is just as horrified by the "modern" way of thinking, according to which a woman marries with the preconceived notion that if anything goes wrong she can easily get a divorce. And Renata is definitely against marriage settlements such as are called in France *"la séparation des biens,"* under which each party retains his own property. Such an agreement prejudices a happy union because it is based on suspicion. She is quick to agree that the possession of wealth by a husband or wife should be regarded as an extra charm in his or her favor.

-- *Chapter 4* --

It was Renata's grandfather who discovered her musical talent. As a child she used to sing at home, not merely hum, but sing, and even then he thought that she had a good ear and a good voice. Renata told me later she heard from Tilde that her grandfather was so convinced of her talent that he spoke to Giuseppina Passani, a piano teacher at the Conservatory in Parma. "I don't know what is going to happen to my Renata," he said, "but I have a feeling that she is going to be somebody in music, and you had better watch her and take good care of her." But her grandfather died when Renata was seven, and for a long time no one else gave another thought to her musical aptitude. Like the other Langhirano children she sang in the church choir, occasionally was given solo parts, and this was as far as it went. Meanwhile she continued the routine life of a schoolgirl for the next six years.

"After I was graduated from the school—I was then thirteen years old—Mamma asked me what I would like to do. I told her that I would like to study music, to learn to play the piano. Mamma seemed to like the idea and she took me to Parma and arranged for me to have lessons with Signorina Passani."

I have met Giuseppina Passani, a charming old lady, who is, I would imagine, in her sixties. I could not succeed in making her say one critical word about Renata. When she speaks of those days when Renata was her pupil, she is so overcome by emotion that tears choke her. Did she think Renata might have become a good or perhaps even a brilliant pianist had she not changed from playing the piano to singing? "Oh, she had such wonderful hands and she is so intelligent," Signorina Passani sighed, closing her eyes.

Passani had been graduated from the Parma Conservatory and although occasionally she played in public, usually at some benefit performance, she then devoted herself to teaching. From what she said I gather that Renata learned everything very quickly, was a good sight-reader, and did not really need to practice as many hours as she did—from four to five hours a day.

The little lady speaks with a very sincere and earnest expression about the way she gives her pupils what she calls a solid technical foundation. She likes to illustrate a point by singing in her thin high-pitched voice. A great admirer of Toscanini, she was trying to explain to me the difference between his interpretation of Beethoven's *Eroica* and that of other conductors. I did not get the point of her argument, but I must admit that I was amazed by the accuracy of her memory and her ability to reproduce themes and certain passages. But as far as Renata was concerned, I did finally manage to find out how far she had progressed under her tutelage. At the time when Renata switched from the piano to singing she was able to play one of Bach's "Three-Part Inventions," a Cramer Étude, and Chopin's "Waltz in C-sharp minor"—a repertoire from which it is much too early to predict anything.

"When I started my lessons with Signorina Passani," Renata reminisced, "every morning I had to take a little dilapidated train to Parma. It consisted of three cars and it took two hours to cover the distance of twenty-five kilometers between Langhirano and Parma. It was a funny train. It looked like one of those you used to have in the West in the United States, which later I saw in the movies. It would stop for a long time at every little village on the way. Perhaps there was no regular schedule, I don't remember, or perhaps they stopped just to chat with their friends at these stations. And when it rained or snowed, because the roofs of the cars were old and cracked, the passengers opened their umbrellas to protect themselves from the water and no one thought anything of it.

"At that time I had a dog. Mico was his name. He was a mongrel and of course very intelligent. He used to accompany me to the train and then return home. When in the afternoon he heard the train whistle he would run out of the house and meet me at the station. But if for some reason or other I was not on the train, he would go back to the house and remain in a corner of the room and would refuse to do anything."

Before Mico Renata had a cat, Bafù. Bafù preferred to spend his time at the store rather than in their apartment. He was a good guardian against strange dogs whom he fearlessly attacked, but he was also a first-class thief. He helped himself to any sausage which hung on the wall within his reach, and he had also learned to open the glass jars containing delicacies which stood in the corners.

"But Bafù scratched me too many times for me to like cats. I prefer dogs." And as Renata was saying this she took into her hands the head of the little French poodle who is always with her wherever she travels now, and out of sheer love she shook it with so violent a passion that I

34

thought the poor thing would breathe his last then and there. Three years ago, after long protests from Giuseppina, Renata finally acquired the puppy one day in New Jersey. She calls him New, derived from New Jersey—not a very imaginative idea, I admit, but the sound is so indistinct that it does not matter much. New turned out to be intelligent, as dogs go, and Renata spoils him terribly, treating him as if he were her little boy.

While studying under Passani, Renata had been daydreaming of becoming a concert pianist. She had no idea how much she would have to know, how long it would take, and how it all was to be accomplished. But she was convinced she could do it, perhaps because she often thought of what her grandfather had predicted. So far she had never even heard a concert pianist: the only musical performance she could remember was an opera. When she was eight years old uncle Valentino had taken her to Parma to see Gaetano Donizetti's *Lucia di Lammermoor*.

The stage with its decor and costumes, and the applause of the public impressed her, but it did not make her wish to become an opera singer. She liked the coloratura best of all and for a while it became her favorite voice. On the day following the performance she tried to sing all the parts she could remember. Later, she added to her repertoire "La donna e mobile" from *Rigoletto*, the tenor's aria "Che gelida manina" from the first act of *La Bohème*, and "Casta diva" from *Norma*. These she had heard on the radio and on records.

She continued to sing this way at home, but as long as she was studying the piano, no one paid much attention to her voice. A few friends did tell Giuseppina that she seemed to sing well and perhaps should study voice instead of the piano, but her mother did not take such advice seriously; in fact without any particular reason she was automatically against it. Renata herself was still thinking of becoming a concert pianist, and perhaps never would have become a singer if it were not for Passani, who made the final decision.

When she heard about Renata's voice she asked her to sing a few arpeggios, scales, and some of her favorite songs and arias. Passani thought that it would be worthwhile to get an opinion and advice from a singing teacher. She spoke about it to Italo Brancucci, one of the voice teachers at the Conservatory in Parma and asked him to hear Renata.

"But what can I sing for him?" Renata asked. "Not Durante's 'Caro mio ben'?" Passani had suggested that she would get the music—Renata was singing everything by ear—and promised to rehearse with her beforehand.

"Brancucci was a singer, and he sang better than he played the piano, but he accompanied me as best he could while he made me sing everything I knew," Renata told me. "It was terrible. I had not the slightest idea of singing. I am surprised at how he could have detected that my voice had a nice timbre, because that was what he said." However, Brancucci told Passani that Renata would have to wait two years before she could even take the entrance examination for the Conservatory. In the Italian music schools they did not accept voice students before they were eighteen years old, and Renata was only sixteen.

This did not dismay the girl. She was big for her age and could easily have been taken for eighteen. In her application Renata simply put down eighteen as her age.

Since Brancucci already had too many pupils, Renata was turned over to Ettore Campogalliani, another voice teacher at the Conservatory, who incidentally was a better pianist than he was a singer. Today he teaches the Master Class at La Scala. But at that time, he had had little experience. Campogalliani was about thirty-seven, tall, slender and "elegant." He wore glasses, had straight black hair, and was adored by his pupils. There were about ten of them in his class in Parma and usually they all remained in the room to listen to each other's lessons. Renata was a beginner and did not shine as an exemplary student. But out of that class she was the only one who has made a professional career.

"It is indeed unfortunate," Renata told me, "that since they have so many voice students, each pupil has three lessons a week lasting only twenty minutes each. I believe it is insufficient. One should have at least one hour a day."

Although I am not a singer, and certainly have no aspirations as a voice teacher, I found what little Renata told me about her opinions on the subject of studying the voice quite interesting.

"Singing must be done in the most natural way. Therefore it should be based on a natural way of breathing. This, of course, is individual, and each student can find out for himself. All he has to do is to lie down on his back and watch where his natural breathing comes from." Renata illustrated to me this simple procedure.

"Once he discovers how he breathes most naturally, he should do it in the same way whether standing or sitting whenever he has to sing. You know," Renata smiled, "one of the teachers in New York once demonstrated to me how he taught his pupils to vocalize while they bent the upper parts of their bodies so that their heads almost touched their knees. To me this makes no sense whatsoever, and I fail to see what such an exercise can achieve.

"As a rule men can breathe from their chests, but it is not right for women. I for instance cannot depend entirely on my diaphragm. I have to support my breath from both sides of the upper part of my body.

"The next problem is how to shape one's mouth in singing. It should be *rotondo,* round. The tongue must be low and not on the palate. The throat must be completely free of any tension, relaxed, and the jaws should not be hard but elastic. If smiling helps a student to relax he should do it, but only occasionally and should not let it become

38

a habit. When he opens his mouth he should have a feeling similar to that of yawning—*sbadigliare*.

"And of course I believe that one of the most important things is for a teacher to explain to his pupil how to hear every note he is singing. One has to be conscious of 'placing' each note in the right way. I don't believe that anyone ever sang just like a bird, not even Tetrazzini or Caruso or Chaliapin. If they did, they were rare exceptions."

It took Renata three months to learn these fundamentals of the art of singing, but only after two years of "training"—vocalizing and doing exercises—was she allowed to learn a few simple songs, written in close intervals, which she could sing for her family and friends. Although she still played the piano she had stopped taking lessons with Passani, and most probably she would have continued to study under Campogalliani until she was graduated, had not pure chance brought about a decisive turn in her schooling. She had just passed her second year at the Conservatory of Parma when she went to Pesaro to spend three weeks of her Christmas vacation with her father's family, her uncle Valentino, and her cousins.

At that time Carmen Melis, an Italian soprano famous for her interpretations of Puccini roles, was teaching at the Pesaro Conservatory. She had retired from the stage after a most brilliant career. Originally from Cagliari in Sardinia, she came from an old aristocratic family. Madame Melis told me that she started to sing very early because everyone in her family sang—her father, an officer in an artillery regiment, had a beautiful baritone, and her mother had a *"superba voce di soprano drammatico"* while her elder brothers also studied music. The theater was my only teacher," she said. "I was born a singer." She must have been one of those rare exceptions Renata had mentioned.

After her debut in Pietro Mascagni's opera *Iris* at the Coccia Theater in Novara, not far from Milan, she had a long operatic career in Italy as well as abroad. In the United States she made her debut in *Tosca* at Hammerstein's Manhattan Opera House in New York, which she followed with appearances in Boston, Chicago, San Francisco, Canada and South America.

In 1941, in her early fifties, she came to Pesaro to teach and often she could be seen visiting a small café because she liked the cakes there. It just happened that the owner of the café was Valentino, Renata's uncle. Valentino must have talked a great deal about his niece to Melis, for finally she told him to bring Renata to her hotel to sing for her.

For the first time in her life Renata learned the meaning of "stage fright"—something dreaded by every artist. For days the thought of singing for the famous Melis gave her a sick feeling, and when the time of her appointment arrived she was trembling like a leaf. Accompanied by her mother, Valentino, and Tilde, she walked into

Melis' apartment in such a nervous state that she doubted that she could sing a note. Everything terrified her—Melis was staying at the "elegant" Albergo Zongo and the solemn atmosphere of the first class hotel intimidated the country girl.

"Now you understand how I felt—you know Madame Melis," Renata explained as she described the scene to me. "Her forbidding appearance frightened me. She looked so sternly at me. Those big black eyes. *Mamma mia!*"

Indeed I can easily see what Renata meant. I remember well my first meeting with Carmen Melis at the apartment in Como where she now lives. She was once a great beauty and even today she is a very impressive lady. She belongs to an era when opera stars and famous actresses were used to living in style, as exotic beings admired by grand dukes and princes. In her sitting room, where large windows give on an enchanting view of Lake Como, one can see many objets d'art and signed photographs of famous composers and conductors of her time as well as of the whole Italian royal family. She has somehow retained the majestic manner which seems to have gone with that era. But beneath her severe aristocratic appearance beats a warm heart, which has earned her the name of Mamma Melis.

Melis listened patiently to Renata's singing "Mi chiamano Mimi" from Puccini's *La Bohème* and "Un bel di" from *Madama Butterfly,* and then told her and her en-

41

tourage of relatives that although Renata did have "good material" to work with, she should not sing that way at all. She referred specifically to Renata's Parma accent, the peculiar "open" pronunciation of all the vowels. Renata in fact sang like the country girl she was. But Melis was kind to her and encouraging, and asked if she would like to work with her during her vacation. Needless to say, Renata and her family were thrilled, and she started on the following day.

One of the first things Melis did was to teach her to sing correctly the arias she had sung for her. Melis would sing them for her in the way they should be sung and then imitate Renata's way to show her the difference. This she repeated with everything Renata knew, so that within five days Renata learned to recognize her faults, particularly in pronouncing such vowels as *a, e,* and *i.* After two weeks of daily lessons Renata was able to sing quite a number of arias and songs, among them Marguerite's waltz aria from Gounod's *Faust.*

"I certainly was impressed by the superb quality of Renata's voice—a *lirico spinto* with a range of two octaves—though she was still only a novice," Melis told me when we spoke about it, "but I was even more impressed by her intelligence and musicianship. She grasped almost instantly everything I told her and in a few days made enormous progress. Before she had to go back to Parma I let her mother come to hear her. Madame Tebaldi was so pleased that with tears in her eyes she embraced and thanked me for what I had done for Renata."

When Renata returned to Parma, her schoolmates and her teacher were astonished—they could not believe it was the same girl singing. "I realized that there was no sense in my continuing working at the Parma Conservatory," Renata said, "and after consulting Mamma I asked to be transferred to the Conservatory at Pesaro."

But Renata's happiness about her studies was marred by a sudden turn in the relationship between her parents. In July of 1940 Italy went to war against the Allies and Teobaldi volunteered for service. He received the rank of captain in the 2nd Grenadier Regiment. At the beginning of the war he was stationed in Parma. There he met Gisella Gasparini, a young widow, with whom it seems he started a love affair.

At first Giuseppina knew nothing about it—she was most of the time in Pesaro with Renata—but eventually she heard the story from friends in Parma and Langhirano. This time it was even more humiliating to her than when she had had to leave her husband before, for it was soon known by everybody that he had deserted for another woman. It was such a blow that several times she tried to commit suicide. Renata remembers that she often would wake up in the middle of the night and would try to feel with her hand whether her mother was still in bed. Once when she discovered that Giuseppina was not there she ran after her. Giuseppina had gone down to the seashore; she intended to drown herself, and only Renata's desperate cries stopped her. At another time she was on the verge of throwing herself out of the window. After these attempts at suicide, if she went on living at all it was for Renata's sake.

"When Mamma discovered that my father was living with that other woman, I went to Parma to see him," Renata told me. "'Ah, your mother is crazy. She is just jealous.' And that was all he said, waving his hand."

I have noticed that even now, after so many years, Renata cannot speak of her father's behavior in a detached way—she becomes very emotional about it. Her extreme devotion to her mother, which some outsiders have considered excessive, Renata explains very simply. "You know," she told me, "how large Italian families usually are, but ours was very small. Perhaps if I too had brothers and sisters, I would not have been so close to my mother, but I had no one except her."

Renata was hurt as much as her mother. She was no longer the child of ten she had been when she first "met" her father. She had begun to understand more than the grown-ups credited her with.

After a while Teobaldi was transferred from Parma to Rome. "But we never heard from him," Renata said. "Someone told us that later he became a prisoner of war and was sent to Corsica. We did not even know whose prisoner he was—the Americans, the British or the French. Mamma was heartbroken. She loved him very

44

much as long as she lived. Had he returned to her after the war, she would still have forgiven him. But he never did. He went back to that woman in Parma, and after Mamma died I heard that he had married her."

After Giuseppina's death Teobaldi wrote to Renata many times but it took years before she was willing to see him. "How could I accept that woman as my mother?" Renata said. "It would be preposterous."

-- *Chapter 5* --

Renata is not only a shy person but she is often moody. Sometimes I would find her looking glum, as if some catastrophe were about to strike us all. I would ask her if anything had happened, if anything were wrong. She would smile and say "No." But I could see that the smile was forced and that in saying no she restrained a sigh. Then it would be of no use to try to bring her out of her depression—she was obviously too preoccupied with her own thoughts, which she kept to herself. But at other times she could be gay. Late one afternoon, shortly before the sun went down over the hills of Rome, she was full of fun as we slowly strolled through the Borghese Gardens. It was one of those rare days in July when a cool breeze from the sea makes summer in Rome bearable.

We were going to have some tea on the terrace of the Casino, but instead Renata pointed at a small clearing in the garden where children were playing and suggested we sit down for a while in the shade nearby. It was touching to see her face light up as she watched their games, or when some of the children passed us, clutching the hands of their nurses tightly. Renata would smile and say a few words to them and then wave goodby with that typical Italian expression: *"Ciao, ciao. . . ."*

As we sat there and chatted, Renata told me that as a girl she had never been particularly good-looking, though "sweet, as children usually are," she said pointing at two little girls who had just passed us. There hadn't been anything exceptional about her, she felt, though of course, her mother had thought she was very beautiful. She had been much too tall and in fact had developed a real complex about it; she had been particularly conscious of her height when playing with other girls of her age. At one time she was even inclined to stoop to make herself seem small, but when Giuseppina had noticed this new habit, it annoyed her and she insisted that Renata hold herself straight.

"I was much too well developed for my age," Renata

said regretfully, "I was *formosa*. But fortunately," she winked at me, "at the age of nineteen or thereabout I changed. But long before that, when I first started working with Madame Melis, at last I met a young man whom I liked. Shall I tell you who he was and how it all happened?" Renata leaned back and for a minute watched the clouds passing over our heads.

"Carlo Migliorati was in the class of Madame Melis. He had a tenor voice and he too hoped to become a singer. He was a typical Italian: tall, slender, with black, black hair and black eyes, and a very dark skin. He was about twenty-five or six, and all the girls in Madame's class were in love with him. And he knew it." Renata laughed. "I fell in love with him instantly, the first time I saw him, but he paid no attention to me, as if he did not see me. I was very jealous of all the girls who had already known him for some time."

Renata readily admits that she is a terribly jealous person—it is her nature, she says, just like her mother's.

"Gradually, however, he began to be more friendly toward me. I knew nothing about men. Many times before I had liked some, but never seriously enough so that they would stop me from thinking about something else. He was the first man who really attracted me, and it made me very happy when finally he took me for a walk, and later on to a movie. We became very good friends."

I knew that this was only the beginning of the story.

"And then?" I asked. "And then . . . " Renata repeated absent-mindedly, "then, one day my cousin Tilde with her fiancé and another girl with her fiancé were going to bicycle to the country for a picnic and they suggested that Carlo and I should join them. Mamma prepared the spaghetti and we took with us some wine and cakes. We stopped at a farm near the Castello di Gradarà. You know the Castello, where Francesca da Rimini lived."

I thought of the great love story as Dante tells it, so romantic that it might have been a legend were it not historically true. It happened about 1285 in Rimini. One of the members of the wealthy and powerful Malatesta family, Giovanni, called the Lame, married the beautiful Francesca, but she fell in love with her brother-in-law Paolo, and when the two lovers were discovered together by Giovanni he murdered them. After we spoke about the tragic fate of Francesca, Renata continued her story.

"We prepared our lunch at a farmer's house, and then feasted on it under a large tree in the park. Later on, the two couples wandered away and Carlo and I were left alone. It was at the end of August; the days were beginning to get short. We walked up the hill and then we sat there and watched the sun go down. Perhaps we spoke about Paolo and Francesca. I don't remember, but it was all very romantic. We watched the clouds in the skies, the birds flew right over our heads, and Carlo told me that he loved me. And . . . he kissed me. This was my first kiss. But please don't laugh at me." Renata lowered her head. "I must admit I was very disappointed. I don't know why, I don't even know what I expected a kiss to be, but I just didn't like it . . .

"However we all returned home in a very good mood, singing as we bicycled back to town. That night I could think of nothing else. I could hardly wait to see Carlo on the following day. For the first time in my life I didn't tell Mamma anything about it. But Carlo began to come so often to see me that Mamma guessed. She did not like the whole thing; she didn't like Carlo. Mamma told me that I was still much too young. I think that really she was jealous of Carlo.

"After that first kiss Carlo again became very reserved and didn't kiss me. Perhaps he sensed that I didn't enjoy it and was afraid to repeat it."

I suggested that when one falls off a horse, the best thing to do is to remount as quickly as possible. "Perhaps he was too young and inexperienced?" I asked.

Renata raised her eyebrows. "Too young and inexperienced at twenty-five? Not in Italy. But it's possible," she continued after a pause, "that I frightened him. I was so serious, forbidding. Perhaps he thought it was much too soon."

"And did it take you a long time to learn to like kissing?" I asked.

Renata laughed. "Not at all. When he finally kissed me again, everything seemed to be all right."

50

Thus began her first flirtation. Renata makes a definite distinction between a "flirt" and something that is more serious. The first one is very innocent, she says. Her "flirt" with Carlo lasted a year and a half. It ended abruptly because he had to leave Pesaro and go somewhere, Renata does not remember where—most probably into the army. After that he never wrote her. Renata did not know much about his family, except that his father was dead and that Carlo lived with his mother and sister. She never met them, and after he left, much later, she heard that while he was in the army he became a Fascist. After the fall of Fascism Carlo was killed by the Partisans.

It was too late for our tea. Renata had to go home and as we walked toward her hotel she told me a little about her life in Pesaro at the time, her studies at the Conservatory and her first public appearance.

In Pesaro Renata and Giuseppina were living at this period with Renata's aunt Giovanna, Teobaldi's sister. She was a widow with four children. She could barely support them on the income from a pastry shop and ice cream stand which she owned. She knew all about her brother's behavior toward Giuseppina and it was natural that the two Tebaldis should stay with her while Renata was studying at the Conservatory. All of them had had a hard time, and Renata learned early that "money does not grow on trees" and that in return for the sacrifices which were made for her studies she should

51

at least do her part and be a good student. Besides, with Melis as her tutor she says it could not have been otherwise.

When I once asked Renata how she had acquired her discipline, whether it was her mother who demanded it of her, she said, "No, it was not Mamma. It was Melis. It was she who taught me the little discipline I have. I had to work very hard or I could not remain as her pupil."

And indeed Renata had a full schedule at the Conservatory. Besides voice she studied theoretical subjects, harmony, even a little bit of counterpoint, and the history of art, and her piano studies continued as well. At the Conservatory she had four lessons a week with Melis, one half hour each, but since Melis believed in her, she also taught her every single day for another hour and a half at her apartment in the hotel.

It was then, while Renata was making such good progress, that she sang for the first time in public.

The concert was to take place in Urbino and she was going to sing "Ebben ne audrò lontan" from Alfredo Catalani's opera *La Wally*, just one number because there were so many other students from the Conservatory who were chosen to participate. But she remembers not so much her new experience as what happened prior to the occasion.

Two nights before, Renata with several other students, including Carlo, of course, went to a music hall in Pesaro where Wanda Osiris, a famous soubrette, was performing. The house was packed and the air was blue with tobacco smoke. They enjoyed themselves and Renata returned home very late. When next morning Melis called up to find out how Renata felt about singing on the following day, Giuseppina had to tell her what had happened. Renata was terribly hoarse. Melis became furious. She called Giuseppina all sorts of names for letting such a thing happen, for even allowing Renata to go out. Terrified, Giuseppina tried to defend Renata, tried to explain, saying that after all she was young and should have some fun once in a while, but this made things still worse. Melis told her that she was a stupid woman and did not understand anything, and she had better put Renata on the phone.

Renata hardly dared open her mouth, but a few words were sufficient for Melis to know what had happened to her voice. She abused Renata even more than she had her mother. She told her to remember once and for all that if she wanted to become a professional singer she must be prepared to lead a different kind of life and certainly should be willing to give up all kinds of pleasures, particularly at a time when she was supposed to sing in public. She finished her tirade by ordering Renata and her mother to get ready immediately—she was going to take them on the first train to Urbino.

During their journey Melis barely spoke to her or to Giuseppina, and as soon as they arrived, she took them to a hotel and called for a doctor. Renata was given two injections and a large basin filled with steaming water. Melis covered her head with towels and told her to inhale.

While Renata was taking this emergency cure Melis kept pacing up and down the room berating the two women. The frightened Giuseppina no longer dared to protest and merely sat silently in a corner. Thus instead of going sightseeing with her colleagues—Urbino is Raphael's birthplace—as Renata had anticipated with so much pleasure, she was put to bed, and Melis stormed out of the room.

On the following day Melis telephoned again to find out how Renata's voice was. The poor girl was afraid to speak to her, but she managed to say that she thought it was getting a little better. "But it is not quite clear yet," Melis said, "you had better come at once to the theater." There, for hours she made Renata vocalize and do her exercises until Melis was satisfied with the sound of her voice.

"This," Renata said, "was my first lesson in becoming a professional—a real singer. It was the lesson of a lifetime."

Ever since then, on the day of any performance Renata avoids talking too much. I must explain that she is not fanatical about it and does not go to extremes, but she definitely guards her voice from any unnecessary strain. She prefers to remain at home and as much as

54

Renata—1927

Renata dressed for her
first Communion

Langhirano—post office and home of the Barbieri family

Mercurio, Milan

Renata returns to Langhirano—1957

Renata with her mother and family—1957

Mercurio, Milan

Program of Renata's first appearance at La Scala,
Arturo Toscanini conducting—1946

Mercurio, Milan

Renata and her former piano teacher, Signora Passani

Mercurio, Milan

Renata and Carmen Melis, her voice teacher

Poggi

Renata as Desdemona, with her mother

Louis Mélançon, New York

Renata as Violetta, with her mother

The young singer: Renata in 1949

On the *Conte Grande*
en route to Rio

Fototecnica, Varese

Varese—1957

Ras, Barcelona

Barcelona—1958

possible alone. She has learned how to control the nervousness sometimes caused by uncalled-for haste. Usually she goes very early to her dressing room in the theater so she can have everything in order in plenty of
time: her costumes, her wigs. She sees to it that everyone who has to work with her while preparing her for
the stage has plenty of time and can work calmly.

On her dressing table she arranges the innumerable
dolls and fetishes which are supposed to bring her good
luck. After making herself up quietly, she prays and
then remains the rest of the time either reading or looking at pictures in magazines. Giuseppina was used to
this procedure, and although she was always with Renata in her dressing room, she never disturbed her with
idle chatter. Renata, like any other performer, is nervous
before a performance, but she has learned to keep her
anxiety in check.

Was she nervous at that first appearance before the
public in Urbino? Renata shook her head. She was more
excited than nervous. She was much too young, she was
only a beginner and she did not have yet the sense of
responsibility which every true artist feels.

At the concert she had a certain amount of success,
but nothing spectacular occurred. Some may have predicted a career, but most of the people in the audience
probably soon forgot her. However, for Renata it was a
memorable occasion. She was flattered to have been

chosen to participate in a concert conducted by Riccardo Zandonai, then the director of the Conservatory in Pesaro, who was also the composer of the opera *Francesca da Rimini* and one of Italy's most prominent musicians.

-- Chapter 6 --

Despite the war Renata continued to study at the Conservatory in Pesaro through 1941 and the first part of 1942. But after November 1942, because of frequent bombing by the Allies the Conservatory was closed.

"Life in Pesaro became difficult for us," Renata said. "I may be mistaken, and you must forgive me if my dates are not always accurate, but I just have a feeling that soon after the Conservatory was closed we all heard about the Partisans, the men who were against Fascism and were pro-Allies. Often members of the same family would be connected with opposing groups and since it was all in dead earnest their lives as well as those of their relatives were not only difficult but dangerous."

For a while Renata continued to work with Melis at her apartment, but when Melis left for Como it no longer made sense for Renata and Giuseppina to remain in Pesaro.

"Since our apartment in Langhirano had been occupied by refugees from the bombed areas, we joined my Aunt Giovanna and her four children and all of us went to live in Cartoceto, a little village some fifteen kilometers away from Pesaro. We lived in a very small apartment, so you can easily imagine that I couldn't do much studying there. But by the end of February even in Cartoceto it was no longer safe and uncle Valentino arranged for a small truck to pick us up and to take us to Traversetolo, another village, this time near Parma, where my Aunt Marianna was staying at the time."

On short notice Giuseppina had to pack whatever she could into two suitcases and the two women, joined by another couple going on to Milan, started at six in the morning on what Renata said was the most perilous journey she ever lived through. They had to drive on roads and through towns and villages which were under constant air bombardment. Often they had to stop and run for shelter until the driver felt it was safe to continue. In this way they went through Rimini, Riccione, Bologna and Parma.

In Traversetolo Renata began to study again alone,

faithfully doing all the exercises Melis had taught her. Fortunately Renzo Martini, a pianist, also had come to Traversetolo with his wife and two children looking for safety. He was happy to work with Renata. There were no pianos to be found in the little village except at the Catholic College for Women, so the two of them had daily sessions there.

In a way Renata was glad to be back near Parma where she had many friends. And, as she said, it was not long before she fell in love, and this time "seriously."

It happened so soon after Carlo left that she did not have much time to miss him. Besides, now that she was really "seriously" in love, she realized that she never had loved Carlo; it had been merely one of those youthful infatuations. They both were students, both were thinking only of their careers, and never spoke of the future in their personal lives. The word "marriage" never crossed their minds. Now it was different.

Antonio Pedretti was a student of medicine at the university in Parma. His family and Renata's had known each other for a long time. In fact Antonio's mother and Giuseppina had been schoolmates. Antonio's father owned some real estate and farms in Banone, a village between Traversetolo and Langhirano. Renata herself had known Antonio for some time, he was her age, but now for the first time they spoke seriously about their future together. In February of 1943 they became officially engaged.

Unfortunately this romance soon ran into difficulties. Antonio joined the Partisans, not as a doctor, but as a regular soldier. Most of the time he was in the hills. He saw Renata only when he could secretly steal into town to see his parents. It was dangerous for him, dangerous for his family, and it was dangerous for Renata because it was known that she was engaged to a Partisan. But Renata bravely walked the two miles from Traversetolo to the mansion of Antonio's father in Banone, where there was enough room for Antonio to hide safely, and where there was a large garden in which their romance was free from any interference. Naturally Renata's sympathies were on the side of her hero's "party." He told her stories of their perilous escapades and Renata was proud of him. And what else did they talk about? What else would two "lovers" talk about? About how much they loved each other.

Giuseppina did not object to Renata seeing him, sometimes as often as three times a week, but she was always worried about it. Giuseppina did not like the Partisans any more than she did the Fascists or the war. She was against the whole thing. But not even Renata knew her thoughts. She kept them to herself. Perhaps Giuseppina blamed her own unfortunate relationship with Teobaldi on the war—if he had not joined the army he might still have been living with them and their lives would have been different.

"Antonio," Renata told me, "was a very good-looking

man, tall, slender, with dark hair and dark eyes, but with a very white skin . . . like mine," Renata pointed to her bare arm. "I know it may sound as if he looked like Carlo, but the fact that his skin was so white gave him a completely different appearance. Like all the Partisans he wore a beard, just like Fidel Castro. It was very becoming to him. But his character was definitely different from that of Carlo. He was proud, stubborn and extremely jealous."

These three qualities are characteristic of Renata's own nature, but she would not be a woman if she did not see them as virtues in herself, while considering them to be vices in a man.

Later, after Italy stopped fighting the Allies and agreed to an armistice, and the Germans occupied the north of the country, the lives of the Partisans became even more perilous. The Germans kept a list of their family names and there was always a danger that some members of the family would be taken as hostages.

Renata, who has a horror of war, having been terrified by the bombings and having seen the devastation it brought to her country and the countless refugees who were shuttling from one place to another seeking safety, remembers particularly how one late afternoon a small detachment of German soldiers arrived in several trucks in Traversetolo. They ordered all the able-bodied men to come to the piazza.

"Through the half-closed shutters we could see the

frightened women running from house to house," Renata described the incident, "and then the poor men—their sons and husbands—go off to the piazza. The Germans packed them into trucks, but they themselves remained in Traversetolo for the night, occupying one of the houses and demanding that food and wine should be brought to them. Later on as they progressed in their feasting they asked for 'girls.'

"But we were all hiding and the Germans were told that the girls were at late evening classes. Perhaps there were other reasons, but they did not do anything about it as far as I know. Next day they departed, carrying off the men, and I have never heard of the fate of those men."

This episode which she witnessed herself, plus everything else she heard and read later about Nazi behavior did not foster in Renata any great love for the German people. And, no doubt, it brought her closer to Antonio and the "cause" for which the Partisans were fighting.

But their engagement dragged on for years, because the better Renata knew Antonio the more she was afraid to marry him. While he was musical himself, he was too jealous to want Renata to become a professional singer.

"I realized that if I was to marry him I would become a mother of many children and that would be all. And I just did not dare to take this step and to forget all the sacrifices which Mamma and I had made on account of my voice. It would have been unfair to Mamma. Also, I didn't feel like giving it up. I had not even started my career, not even given it a fair chance. Besides I loved music."

"And how did Mamma feel about it?" I asked.

"Mamma was very unhappy about my decision. She liked Antonio very much."

Perhaps Giuseppina was too anxious about all the difficulties connected with a musician's career and felt that Renata was neglecting the chance of a good marriage with a comfortable life in prospect.

And as if to remind Renata that she had already made her choice, she received a letter at this time from Carmen Melis asking her if she would like to make her debut in an opera. Arrigo Boito's *Mefistofele* was going to be given in May in Rovigo. She would sing not Margherita's part but that of Elena or Helen of Troy, the Greek beauty of the classical scene. It was going to be conducted by Giuseppe Del Campo, one of the foremost opera conductors in Italy at that time.

The beginning of Giuseppe Del Campo's musical career was similar to that of Arturo Toscanini. Like Toscanini he was born in Parma, also studied the cello at the same Conservatory, and went twice to play as a cellist in the orchestras of the opera houses in South America. Then, like Toscanini, he switched from playing cello to conducting. He made his debut with Umberto Giordano's opera *Andrea Chenier* in Parma in 1915, after which he conducted for several years in the opera houses in northern Italy. In the twenties his conducting of Giuseppe Verdi's *Il Trovatore* at the Teatro Donizetti in Bergamo so impressed Toscanini, who was present at the performance, that he helped his younger colleague in the development of his career. When Toscanini left La Scala, Del Campo took his place. He was particularly well-known for his interpretations of Verdi and the other Italian opera composers of the nineteenth century.

Even if Renata were still wavering in her decision about her career, she could not have resisted such an opportunity.

Melis told Renata to come to Rovigo ten days before the rehearsals so she could work with her and prepare her for the performance. Many months had passed since Renata had seen Melis, but when Melis heard her she was rather pleasantly surprised. Renata's working without her had done her no harm, and soon Renata had mastered the part of Elena to Melis' satisfaction.

On the night of the performance Melis came to the theater to make up Renata, help her with her costume, and to remain with her up to the last minute before she had to go on the stage. In her role as Elena Renata was revealed reclining on a couch as the curtain went up for the fourth act. Only after Melis was entirely satisfied with Renata's pose did she signal to the stage manager that the scene could start. She herself retired into the wings.

"This was my first appearance in an opera and I was

frightened to death," Renata told me. "I was terribly nervous; still, as long as Mamma Melis was with me before the curtain rose I could control myself. But after she left, and the footlights were turned up, and I could hear the audience returning to their seats after the intermission, could hear the sound of their voices, I practically lost my head. It threw me into a panic. I don't remember now what it was that crossed my mind like lightning, but I felt I couldn't endure it another minute and I was going to run away. I had already lifted myself on my arms from the couch when suddenly I saw two large black eyes piercing through me. They were the eyes of Melis—she was facing me from the wings and I heard her whisper: 'Don't you dare to move!'

"It paralyzed me. I would have fainted if at that very moment the curtain had not gone up and I had to start singing the duet with Pantalis. In a flash of a second it sobered me up. I still felt nervous only while singing the first few phrases, and as I went on I recovered completely and forgot all about Melis, Mamma, and the large audience—I thought only of the music I was singing and the role I was playing."

Although Melis was pleased with her, there was no special celebration of Renata's debut. After the performance Melis, Del Campo, Giuseppina and Renata returned to the hotel and had a quiet supper.

Actually Renata does not consider this evening as the real beginning of her operatic career, because, as she points out, it was not followed by other performances. Later, in the fall of the same year (1944) she sang in *La Bohème* in Parma. This performance was organized by Martini, the pianist with whom she used to work in Traversetolo. He had gathered a group of local singers and the opera was given in the Teatro Ducale, a cinema in the old part of the town. A year later she sang again in Parma in *La Bohème, L'Amico Fritz,* and *Andrea Chenier,* but all these appearances were far apart, she said.

I suspect that the true reason why Renata does not consider these performances as the beginning of her operatic career lies in the fact that the audiences were rather divided in their opinion—some predicted a future for her, but others did not. Renata would have to be completely lacking in vanity if she did not prefer to choose a happier occasion. Two years later, in 1946, she sang Desdemona in Verdi's *Otello* in Trieste and she was unanimously acclaimed. This she believes was the true beginning of her career.

After her Rovigo performance, Melis suggested that she had better come to study some more with her. With financial help from their relatives and friends Renata and Giuseppina went to Milan. Antonio, who knew the city, found a room in Signora Poccinesta's apartment on Via Broggi for them—the room where they later stayed again when Renata returned for her audition with Toscanini.

Milan was the first large city Renata had seen. She told me once that she was just as impressed by Milan then as she was later on by New York City. She was impressed by the large Cathedral, the Piazza, but above all by the crowds of people in the streets, all rushing about their business—something she had never seen before, not in Langhirano, nor in Parma, nor Pesaro.

"The first thing I did after we arrived in Milan was to go to see La Scala. I walked by myself to the square in front of it and there I remained for a long time just looking up in awe at the beautiful building."

Later on, Renata was taken inside of the opera house. La Scala had been bombed during the war and the ceiling was badly damaged. It happened that during those first days in Milan it rained practically all the time and Renata's heart ached as she saw the water pouring through the roof onto the floor and the seats of the famous theater.

Renata soon realized how small her repertoire was: she knew only *La Bohème, Andrea Chenier, Mefistofele, L'Amico Fritz*, and *Otello*. This was far from enough for an opera singer. She had a great deal to learn, and she went three times a week to Melis' apartment in Como. One day when Melis had come to Milan she happened to be seeing her off at the station in Milan when Melis saw a friend, a Madame Pais, there. Her husband was a well-known operatic coach. Originally Giuseppe Pais, who now lives in Milan, had come from Venice. The son of a professor at the Venice Lyceum, Pais began his musical education at the age of seven at the local Conservatory. He wanted to become a composer and indeed was graduated in 1909 from the Conservatory's class of composition, but instead became a conductor both of opera and symphonic works. He was often heard at La Scala and at the Teatro Costanzi, now the opera house of Rome, but World War I interrupted his career for almost six years. Although he continued to conduct he became better known as a vocal teacher and a coach and today is considered among the foremost in Italy.

Melis herself had studied many roles with Pais, and she felt that Renata could not have a better coach. Besides, and this Melis told me, she had chosen Pais because he was happily married to his former pupil, a charming young Russian, and it was safe to trust him with Renata. It seems to be a forgone conclusion that when students are beautiful girls, Italian voice teachers do more lovemaking than teaching. Thus, while continuing her work with Melis, Renata also had daily lessons with Pais. She worked with him for six years. (In the spring of 1947, in Catania, Pais conducted Renata's first *Tosca*.)

Pais has told me that Renata was one of his most diligent pupils. She had, he said, an incredible determination, and by autumn of 1944 she was ready to audition for Guido Gatti, then the superintendant of La Scala. But Gatti could not do much for her because toward the end of the war no performances were given at La Scala. A year later, in September of 1945, Renata auditioned for Liduino Bonardi, the well-known artist and concert manager in Italy. Bonardi offered her a contract. It was sort of a scholarship which she was to repay later from her fees. She was to receive five thousand lire per month (about eight dollars at that time). Usually these managers would drive a hard bargain with their protegés and sometimes even exploit them for a long time, but Renata told me that Bonardi always acted like a gentleman and he remains her manager to this day.

It was Bonardi who arranged for Renata to sing in Brescia in May 1946, before she returned to Milan to see Toscanini.

"A few days after my audition for Maestro," Renata told me, "Oldeni called me up and asked me to come to see him at his office in La Scala. He said he had something important to tell me. I ran to La Scala. From the extremely courteous way Oldeni treated me, helping me into a chair, bowing and smiling, I guessed that my audition with the Maestro must have been successful. And indeed it had been, Oldeni told me. The Maestro had chosen me for his concert for the reinauguration of La Scala. This was the reason why Oldeni wanted to speak to me. He told me that I must at once learn an aria from Rossini's opera *Mosè in Egitto,* and a small part in Verdi's *Te Deum,* the score of which Oldeni showed me.

"And now I must tell you something that may disappoint you. Or should I let you believe a fable which grew out of a simple misunderstanding?" Renata looked almost mischievous.

"No, I feel I must tell you the truth. You see, right at the first rehearsal the Maestro was very much impressed when after the trumpet takes an E natural, I followed it with the same note and in exactly the same timbre. The Maestro said that this note should sound as if it came from heaven, and therefore during the performance I was placed high above the chorus. It was this remark of Toscanini about the sound of the voice which should be like that of an angel from heaven that started the story, according to which he said that I had a voice like an angel."

On the night of the performance La Scala was filled with a brilliant audience. The people were saying all Milan was there. Ovation followed ovation. This was all, Renata said, that she could remember. The event was too overwhelming for her—"When the performance was over I was dead."

"Do you at least remember if you sang that note well?" I asked.

"Oh . . . of course I did. To Maestro that note in the exact timbre meant more than the whole of 'O patria mia,' the aria of Aida on the Nile."

-- Chapter 7 --

After the war ended Renata's fiancé Antonio returned to his study of medicine at the University in Parma. During those years he used to come to see Renata wherever she happened to be, in Milan, Traversetolo, or Langhirano. He wrote her letters constantly. Renata also wrote him, but not as often, perhaps twice a week, she said. But as time went on she found herself less and less interested in his letters. In fact they did not make her happy, and she no longer looked forward to receiving them. Antonio was much too preoccupied with psychoanalysis and wrote her

71

too many serious letters on that subject. He also began to analyze Renata, far too much, she thought. It did not seem to foster their romance and the ties of their engagement grew thinner. When during the summer of 1947 Antonio came with his mother to Verona, where Renata was singing at the festival, she was already in love with somebody else. Antonio understood and left. This was the end of their engagement.

Later Antonio had many love affairs with other women, and although Renata was in love with someone else, still she was jealous, she admits. But now it is all forgotten, at least on Renata's side. Antonio has remained a bachelor, and Renata thinks that perhaps he would still like to marry her, but she is no longer interested in him. She repeats that it was difficult for her to make the choice between her career and marrying him, and that she suffered a great deal in making this decision. But the final break was not hard because she fell in love with a man, a singer like herself, with whom she had far more in common, and she was extremely happy.

Renata met Nicola Rossi-Lemeni, the basso, in Verona where both of them were singing in Gounod's *Faust:* he as Mephistopheles and she as Marguerite. They fell in love almost instantly, at the first rehearsal. After the second rehearsal Nicola sent her an enormous bouquet of flowers with a card: *"From Mephisto to Marguerite."*

Nicola was about Renata's age, or perhaps a year younger. He was born in Constantinople. His parents came there as refugees from Russia. Originally an Italian, Nicola's father had gone to live in Russia, where he married Xenia Makedon, who at one time was a vocal teacher at the Odessa Conservatory. Today he is a retired colonel of the Italian army.

"There is so much interesting to see in Verona and Nicola was a wonderful guide," Renata once told me. "He knew so much about everything—I think he was educated in Verona, perhaps he had studied law there. I don't remember. But he knew a lot about history, literature, and history of art. At that time he was particularly interested in paintings and I was fascinated by his stories and descriptions. Our conversations, as you see, were always on a high intellectual plane." Renata smiled. "Everyone who saw us walking arm-in-arm on the streets of Verona used to remark what a handsome couple we were."

There is a popular legend about a beautiful fountain in the garden of the Teatro Romano in Verona, according to which, if a boy and a girl bend down and look at their reflection in the water they are bound to fall in love. The stage director at the Festival, whose name Renata has forgotten, suggested this to them, but Nicola and Renata laughed—they were already in love.

They were so blissfully happy that they did not need to visit Juliet's supposed tomb, to hold hands there while making a wish, which according to another superstition would come true. When I reminded Renata of the tomb's

73

magic power, she somehow did not seem to regret that they had missed that opportunity. For she told me that soon after the beginning of their relationship she realized what the main obstacle was. It was Nicola's mother, Xenia.

Renata thought that Xenia was always a most dignified lady, but very haughty. Xenia claimed to be related by blood to the Romanoffs. She was willful, particularly in whatever concerned her son, jealous of him, and always a strong character. Nicola had to do just what Xenia wanted. Despite his age, he had to be home at the time she expected him for lunch and dinner, and he must never be late in the evenings. Nicola complained about it to Renata but apparently was unwilling to do anything about it. And to make things worse, Xenia did not think that Renata and her background were good enough for her son. She had met Giuseppina and may have made her snobbish attitude apparent to Signora Tebaldi. Giuseppina, however seemed to like her and never said an unkind word about her to Renata. Besides, she was much too preoccupied with taking care of her daughter in the small apartment they had rented. Giuseppina preferred it to staying at a hotel as they usually did.

Renata and Nicola spent a happy month in Verona. Then again for a month she saw him in Florence, where Nicola was singing in Moussorgsky's *Khovantchina,* and Renata in Wagner's *Lohengrin.* And they were again together in Rome: at the Baths of Caracalla they sang in

74

Boito's *Mefistofele*. However, much as they thought they were in love with each other, they never spoke of marriage. They were primarily interested in their careers and their happy relationship apparently included no plans for their personal future. Although this flirtation was important to her, I do not believe there was ever a question of marrying Nicola in Renata's mind. At any rate life itself gave them the answer. Two years later, while he was in Rome Nicola fell in love with Vittoria, the daughter of the well-known Italian conductor Tullio Serafin.

Vittoria, so the story goes, had had much experience for her age. She had traveled a great deal, always accompanying her father on his tours, and had become quite sophisticated. She was older than Nicola, and had been married twice before he met her. Her first marriage had been annulled; by her second husband she had two children. Eventually she divorced him in Mexico. When Nicola went to sing at the Colon in Argentina, Vittoria followed him. It must have been flattering to him. He fell desperately in love with her.

"I can easily understand this," Renata explained to me. "She was a woman of the world and this appealed to him. He was young and immature in these matters."

Xenia was very unhappy about her son's *liaison* with Vittoria, but this time she did not seem to be able to do much about it. When Renata finally heard from her friends about the affair, she wrote Nicola that if the rumor was true, she considered it ended their relationship, and that she felt free to return to Antonio. Actually she did not go back to her fiancé. She only said this and suffered in silence. Usually her mother was her confidante and she had talked to her about Nicola when she was happy and when she had her doubts, but this time she said nothing and only mentioned it to Giuseppina after she had already mailed the letter.

Nicola showed no particular reaction to her decision— that was the end of their romance.

I have asked Renata whether today, in retrospect, she thinks that she acted wisely, whether perhaps she should have forgiven Nicola if he had returned to her, as for instance, her mother had done when Teobaldi had come back to live with them. Still proud of her decision, Renata haughtily said, "No." She was very emphatic about it. She said she could never share a man with anyone. She is much too proud—*troppo orgoglioso*. She repeated that she is very jealous, but that is her nature, she said, and there is nothing she can do about it.

"Well then," I persisted, "would you have reconsidered your decision if after Nicola had received your letter, he had dropped everything he was doing, left his engagements at the opera, left Vittoria, left his mother, and hurried back to you?"

"Ah, but he did not," Renata said with her disarming smile.

"And what did your mother say?" I asked.

"Mamma tried to comfort me. I think that she always thought that in the long run it would not work because of Nicola's mother. She made her attitude toward us much too obvious."

"And I suppose she told you men are like that?" I asked.

Renata nodded, and gave me a long look as if to say: "And what did you expect Mamma to say?" Giuseppina had learned this from her own bitter experience.

When Nicola returned from Argentina with Vittoria whom he meanwhile had married, Vittoria would not even greet Renata. But later on when she realized that it was all over between Renata and Nicola she became more gracious. They never spoke of what happened and the subject was mutually considered as closed. Finally Renata said to me that she too, like her mother, came to the conclusion that it probably never would have worked out anyway and that made it easier for her to get over it.

Renata did not explain what she meant by "It wouldn't have worked out anyway." She did not have to.

Renata had no reason to be ashamed of her background. And if in meeting Xenia and her friends she was introduced for the first time in her life to the so-called upper class, she could easily see how much certain members of the *bel mondo* had to be modest about rather than proud. Renata, endowed with a sober intelligence, was far from condemning an entire class on the basis of the superficiality of a few, but it was a different world indeed.

Eventually she understood their ways of living, reasoning and judging others, which were often based on purely material considerations.

Although she was willing to adopt some of the ways of the *bel mondo*—being a young woman she learned quickly to appreciate fashionable clothes and jewelry, and to prefer the beautiful rather than the utilitarian in her surroundings—her morality and her sense of right and wrong remained unshaken. She was duly impressed by the fanciful stories of past grandeur and lost estates, but she has never developed an appreciation of the ways in which the niceties of a certain etiquette can smooth the path of even a great artist. Having read little Renata was only vaguely acquainted with other people's lives. She resented having her background considered inferior, and her pride made her cling harder to it rather than renounce it.

Still being very young, had Renata lived alone she might have learned to be superficially gracious, to say sweet nonsense she did not mean, and to flatter against her better judgment. But she lived always with her mother, whom she worshipped. Giuseppina stood for her as a model of the virtuous woman, who at great sacrifice and with very modest means had managed to give her daughter the necessary education for her career and to make her the honest person she was. Renata and her family knew no self-pity, the word poverty was not mentioned, they were contented with what they had. Also,

Renata had no reason to think her mother loved her less than Xenia did her son, but Giuseppina was not as selfish as Xenia was. She seemed to Renata far wiser—if there is such a thing as happiness Giuseppina probably understood it better than the *bel mondo*.

Since that abortive romance Renata has seen more of the world; in fact she has seen all there is to see of "society," and I have a feeling that she never would care to make a great success in that particular sphere. Always she will prefer Mamma's way. It is imbedded as in a rock, and she is perfectly happy with it.

All this I have gathered from many talks I have had with Renata, but while discussing her relationship with Nicola, I often preferred to ask her more specific questions. For instance, did she really get over this romantic affair? Renata is very easily impressed by a man's appearance. Men's clothes mean a great deal to her. She often uses, as I have said before, the word "elegant" in describing men. She still remembers a concert at La Scala at which Nicola sang in four different languages. She remembers particularly one Russian song about political prisoners in Siberia. But she was far more profoundly impressed by the way Nicola looked in his evening dress suit. Speaking of it she said with pride: "He looked like a *Signore*."

I have a feeling that Nicola came closer than anyone else to Renata's idea of the sort of man her husband should be.

I must admit that knowing Renata as well as I do, I was surprised by the candid way she spoke to me of these personal things. Renata is a closed-in person in many ways. Except for the extraordinary attachment to her mother, Renata had and has no intimate friends, and by an intimate friend I mean someone to whom she would confide whatever goes on in her heart and mind. Even when some of her friends sometimes feel that at last they have crossed the barrier which separates them from her, they are apt to find the next day that they are no closer to her than they were before. On first meeting a stranger Renata is always reserved, almost on the defensive. She knows her own worth, and perhaps also she realizes some of her failings. Her manner is dignified, even cold until she begins to feel at ease and then all the warmth of her personality is shown in her charm. She is intelligent and honest. There is not one ounce of calculated shrewdness in her and when she sees through somebody or something she smiles with a childish surprise at her own cleverness.

Like any other woman she is pleased to receive compliments, but flattery leaves her cold, and perhaps even a bit suspicious. These qualities are inherent in her as in most *enfants du peuple*. But, at the same time, she has not yet assimilated certain conventional ways of behavior, and this is often held against her. When giving a dinner party Renata is capable of having her chauffeur take a place at the table next to her guest of honor. She means no harm, nor offense to the guest—she just does not realize that such "democratic" ways may appear to some rather plebeian. However, her charm and gracious manner in direct relationships defeat criticism and those who meet her soon overlook her occasional lapses in etiquette.

Renata told me that she sometimes thinks she has a split personality. When she is on stage, she says, she is entirely dominated by the character of the conductor or the stage director. As examples she mentioned Toscanini and Victor de Sabata. Then, she says, she is as meek as a lamb. But in her private life no one, so far, has been able to dominate her. Perhaps it is a consequence of her childhood, the relationship between her parents, their poverty, and later on her early independence and her work, where she had to learn to stand on her own. And of course first of all there is her pride. All this she thinks made her what she is.

"But do you think I am an egoist?" she once asked me, and I felt that she is a bit afraid of that word. Perhaps she had heard that some people think she is.

"Men, real men," Renata concluded, "cannot be dominated."

"But have you met a real man?" I asked. "So far you have been in love with boys in their twenties."

"Perhaps you are right," she was quick to agree. "Then I certainly do hope that one day I shall meet a real man."

And this will be the man Renata will marry. For she has said that she has no intention of remaining single for the rest of her life. But she has very definite ideas about

81

marriage. She does not believe that she can combine it with her career, because marriage means to her a family life. She would like to have children and she does not see how she could then leave her family and go for the greater part of the year traveling all over the world. When she marries she must give up singing in public. It will be a great sacrifice, but now that she has made a great career she would be ready to do it.

Once when we were on this subject I asked her if it is true that in Italy some people adhere to the old-fashioned idea that women connected with the theater have lower moral standards than others. She said that this is unfortunately still true, but, she explained, there is a good reason for it. Women in the theater work constantly with men; in the roles they play they are emotionally involved with their partners, and the frequent proximity of men offers more temptations than are present in other professions. And this, she thinks, may be one of the many other reasons why men are not too anxious to marry women of the theater.

As if we were playing a game I asked her what sort of man she would like her husband to be.

"First of all," she said, "I would not like him to be just a Prince Charming, who could accompany me everywhere. Nor would I like him to be Mr. Tebaldi. He has to be *somebody*, somebody on his own. Think of how many singers and actresses I know whose husbands' names I can't even remember."

82

She said that he should have some kind of a profession
—she would not care what kind: an engineer, a doctor, a
professor, but he must have one at which he works. She
could not think of marrying a rich man who does not do
anything. "Those men have no aim in life, and it is dis-
astrous how it affects their characters," she said.

I asked Renata to tell me some of the other qualifica-
tions for a future suitor. "First, he must be at least as tall
as I am." She is very conscious of her height, which is five
feet eight. "But he must not be much taller than I am.
That would be too much."

She did not attempt to describe his looks. We took it for
granted that of course there would be nothing repulsive
about him.

"He must be intelligent and well educated," she continued.

I knew it was impertinent of me, but since it was a
game, I risked asking her what she would discuss with a
well educated man—her own erudition being far from
wide.

Renata did not mind my question. "I would listen to
him and learn," she said shyly. "He would have to have
an even temper and a great deal of patience," she went
on, after a pause. By this she was perhaps acknowledging
that her own character was not one of the easiest to live
with.

"And if he was a musician I would make him play for
me for hours every day." From the coquettish look she

gave me I saw that she was playing her part of the game —up to this moment I could claim that I myself would fit the requirements for her suitor. But before I had a chance to say so, she raised her forefinger, as if triumphantly winning the game and said, "Ah, but of course, before anything else he has to be an Italian."

She also told me that she could never live with anyone who would want to be with her all the time, smothering her with his affection. This I did not believe, but I saw no sense in arguing with her, nor would I with any other woman. On this point I only succeeded in making her confess that perhaps she had not yet experienced true love.

-- Chapter 8 --

On June 26, 1949 Toscanini was going to conduct Verdi's *Requiem* at La Scala and Luigi Oldeni had engaged Renata for this performance. Evidently she had sung well at her first concert with the Maestro. Besides her he engaged Giacinto Prandelli, Fedora Barbieri, mezzo-soprano (no blood relation to Renata's mother), and Cesare Siepi, the basso.

"It was very exciting to have rehearsals with the Maestro," Renata said. "At first we worked in the Yellow Room with an accompanist, but when Maestro felt that we were ready, he started us with the orchestra. Maestro was very happy to work with us because we were all very young, full of enthusiasm, and eager to please him. He had a sort of hypnotic power—often I could sense what he wanted before he asked for it."

The performance was a tremendous success. This time Renata bashfully said it was not only because of Toscanini—the audience was curious about the progress of these young artists, and, of course, of Tebaldi. After the concert Antonio Ghiringhelli, the director of La Scala, gave a large supper party at his home. All the dignitaries of Milan, the old aristocrats and everyone of importance were invited. Renata with the rest of the cast was placed at a table with Toscanini, Ghiringhelli, and the Mayor of Milan. In his honor, Toscanini was served his favorite dish, a risotto with a meat sauce, a Parma specialty.

This was Renata's first big party. Since it was held right after the concert she had no time to go home to change and she wore the same dress she had worn on the stage: a simple, slim dress of heavy black silk with touches of white lace at the high neck and long sleeves. She wore no jewelry, and her hair, long, as she wore it at that time, fell in waves on her shoulders.

At the table Renata was seated next to Toscanini and while he chatted with her he asked about her repertoire. He was surprised that she did not sing *Aida*. She told him that she thought the part of Aida was for a dramatic soprano, particularly the first two acts, and only the third

86

and the last act were written for a purely lyric soprano. But Toscanini said it was all a matter of "accent." He asked her to come to see him at his home; he would, he said, explain it to her.

A few days later, accompanied by her friend Madame Carmen Scalvini, Renata went to Toscanini's apartment on Via Durini.

Carmen Scalvini at that time had begun to take a great interest in Renata's career and the two women had become close friends. Originally Scalvini was a singer herself. She came from Puerto Rico and was at one time married to the brother of Mattia Battistini, a well-known baritone. Now she is married to Giuseppe Scalvini, who heads the largest artists' agency in Italy. Until a few years ago Madame Scalvini used to have an "at home" every Friday evening. Artists and Milan society used to gather there. It was Madame Scalvini who introduced Renata to Milan society, which, while it entertained Renata momentarily, left no particular impression on her. It did not change her life in any way. But now Madame Scalvini no longer has her *jour fixe*.

Carmen Scalvini discreetly left Renata with the Maestro and went to talk to Signora Toscanini in an adjoining room.

Renata remembers well the studio in his nine-room apartment, where Toscanini went straight to the piano and opened the score of *Aida*. A large rug covered the floor, and all around the room were shelves with music and books. She noticed several original paintings: Stragliati's portrait of Verdi on his deathbed, Victor Grubicy's landscape of Lago Maggiore and Telemaco Signorini's *La Toiletta del Mattino*. There were also several busts: Verdi, Catalani and two by Troubetskoy in bronze: one of Puccini and the other of the Maestro. Still she felt that the atmosphere of this room was rather austere. Maestro did not like too much light in his studio and it was kept somber by heavy draperies and curtains.

"This was the first time I saw him at home," she told me. "He always wore the same loosely hanging black tunic with a high collar. On his right wrist he wore a thin gold bracelet with all kinds of good-luck pieces. They jingled as he gesticulated."

Accompanying himself on the piano Toscanini sang in a high-pitched voice most of the soprano part in *Aida*, showing Renata how by a mere "accent" she could overcome the difficulties in the first two acts. By an "accent" he meant what is called *accento-declamato*, which should be achieved by pronouncing every single syllable as clearly and as *marcato* as possible. Since the part of Aida is very long he advised beginning rather carefully— *adagio*, as he said—thus saving the voice for the rest of the opera. Otherwise, he maintained, it would be difficult for a singer to carry on.

During the following season Ghiringhelli asked Renata if she would like to sing Aida at La Scala. She made her debut on February 12, 1950 in the part with Mario del

Monaco and Fedora Barbieri. It was conducted by Antonio Votto and she had a great success.

This was the beginning of a most valuable and happy relationship with one of the major opera houses in the world. When later Renata spoke of herself as a true "creation" of La Scala she merely stated a biographical fact.

In the spring of 1950 Renata received an invitation to come to America to sing at the San Francisco Opera. She was engaged for the opening of the following fall season and the contract came directly from Gaetano Merola, then the general manager of the San Francisco Opera. Merola had never been content to present only the established Met stars—he had already introduced an unusually large number of new voices and had justified his choice in every instance. A Neapolitan and an accomplished musician himself, he may have heard Renata in Italy, but Renata thought that his decision to bring her to San Francisco was based on her recordings.

Renata started the fall season that year by going with the La Scala company (Prandelli, Barbieri, and Siepi among others) to the Edinburgh Festival. There, accompanied by the orchestra of La Scala conducted by Victor de Sabata, they sang Verdi's *Requiem*. This was followed by two performances of *Otello* at Covent Garden in London, after which she took a plane with her mother to San Francisco via New York.

On this first trip to the United States she saw nothing

of New York, except for Idlewild Airport, where she had some difficulty in explaining the nature of her work to the immigration authorities. Renata's English was clear and understandable: with a slight accent she could say "thank you," "please be seated," "hello," and "good-bye" —but nothing else. The immigration officers did not know a word of Italian. Thus it took some time before they understood each other, and only after she produced her contract was she allowed to proceed as far as the Newark Airport, where she and her mother were to board a plane for San Francisco.

While they were traveling through the Holland Tunnel Renata was told that they were traveling under the Hudson River and this made her terribly nervous. Suddenly all sort of scenes from the films in which torrents of water engulfed everything flashed through her mind. She was convinced that somehow the water would pour through the cracks into the tunnel and all of them would drown. I do not believe that to this day Renata understands why they could not travel by land, or over a bridge, or did not land in New Jersey instead of at Idlewild.

Renata has always been terrified of flying and although the trip from London had been comfortable and uneventful she could hardly wait for the end of the journey. But luck was against her. On the way to San Francisco their plane had engine trouble and they had to land in Denver and wait for two hours there before they could get on another plane. It was four in the morning when they finally arrived in San Francisco and were taken to the Whit-comb Hotel on Market Street. Both she and Giuseppina fell into their beds completely exhausted from the ordeal.

When next day Renata was going out to take a look at the city about which she had heard so much, her attention was caught by a man of an unusual height who was standing in the lobby of the hotel. He must have been at least six feet four inches tall. But what surprised her even more was that right after she saw him, she saw another man just as tall, if not taller, then still another, and then a whole group of such men talking loudly, gesticulating and obviously enjoying something Renata could not understand.

The mystery of this unusual sight was solved for her by one of her colleagues, an Italian singer, who happened to walk into the hotel. He explained to Renata that these giants were the members of an organized "Congress of Tall Men and Tall Women of the State of California." And indeed, later on, Renata saw a great number of women of similar height. Both men and women were of all ages, young and old, and they seemed to have completely taken over the hotel where Renata was staying. The lobby, the hall and the dining room were filled with them and their loud laughter, and it was quite an art for Renata and her mother to reach their table without stumbling over their legs.

"You know I am not a small girl myself," Renata smiled,

"but this was terrifying. And the women? I have never seen such large feet."

But this was only the beginning of Renata's adventures in the new city. After taking a short walk she and her mother returned to their room to have a rest for a few hours—they were still very tired from the journey. Then, at about eight in the evening they came down to have their dinner. They were told that the kitchen had been closed since seven-thirty. This the two Italian women, used to dining at eight or even later in the evening, could not understand. They were puzzled but there was nothing to do about it. They were afraid to go out by themselves looking for a restaurant. Earlier in the day they had seen no restaurants in the vicinity of the hotel—only a few drug stores with counters, coffee shops and bars, crowded with what seemed to them strange-looking men. Renata said frankly that they were afraid of these places and preferred to remain in their room. Luckily they had had a good lunch and what was even more fortunate, Carl Weber, the manager of the hotel, had been thoughtful enough to leave a bowl of fruit in their room, though he, of course, was completely unaware of their predicament.

By chance the same thing happened on the following day. This time Renata tried to get hold of Mr. Weber, but he was away for the day and she was too shy to approach anyone else. The Tebaldis would have gone for three days without dinner if on the third day Madame del Monaco had not come to their rescue. She found Renata sitting in bed weeping—she was so hungry, she complained. Madame del Monaco immediately took Giuseppina to the nearest supermarket, and from then on they always had plenty of food in their room in case of emergency. Ever since, Renata has had a warm spot in her heart for American supermarkets.

Once this very important problem was solved Renata became an avid sightseer. She loved San Francisco. It seemed to her like a fairyland, with beautiful views of the mountains, the ocean, the bay, the streets with their cable cars, the zoo, and, of course, Chinatown. Although they spent a whole month in San Francisco, she was, she said, unfortunately taken there only twice with other members of the opera company. She did not dare to venture there alone with her mother. She tasted the authentic Chinese dishes; she liked particularly the way they prepared pigeons and all sorts of vegetables. Renata was so curious about it that later on, after dinner, she insisted on being taken down to the kitchen to watch the Chinese cook. To her amazement she found they steamed the vegetables instead of boiling them.

During those first days before her debut, she spent most of the time at the opera house rehearsing. Since I was not present at the performance I shall quote from a report by Alfred Frankenstein, the music critic of the San Francisco *Chronicle*. He has heard so much music in his life that he can afford to be blasé about almost any performance. This time, however, even he must have been impressed.

Tuesday evening it seemed as if the intermission crowd was a little thicker than usual, that more people stepped on my feet in the lobby than is customary on Flashbulb Night, that the parade of gowns and boiled shirts was more stimulating than it sometimes has been, and that the whole crowded, lavish, jewel-studded occasion was really an event to be enjoyed. For even the most confirmed of old-time newspaper cynics would warm toward an event which included—even if incidentally—so thoroughly splendid a performance of *Aida* as that which Fausto Cleva conducted, starring Renata Tebaldi, Mario Del Monaco, Elena Nikolai, Robert Weede and Italo Tajo.

Frankenstein then joined his confreres, the other critics, in praising Renata. They were merely repeating what had been already said many times, that she has a miraculous voice which combines dramatic fervor with an exquisitely pure tone, whatever the volume of the sound, and an ethereal quality. And speaking of Renata's ability to use this extraordinary instrument, a typical review said that "phrase and nuance are exactly what Mme Tebaldi possesses in highly generous measure."

After Renata's second San Francisco appearance, this

time as Desdemona in *Otello,* they were convinced that it would be necessary to go back to Claudia Muzio before they would meet again such a phenomenon. (Claudia Muzio was the world-famed soprano who died in 1936.) And indeed some reporters even asked Renata if she were aware of the resemblance. Renata admitted that she had listened to many of Muzio's recordings, but she sees little similarity in her singing and Muzio's. Unless, she added, in the *pianissimo,* or a certain manner of expressing emotion. Actually Muzio, like Renata, was a *lirico spinto* soprano who sang dramatic roles because of her ability in dramatic enunciation.

"Muzio was Muzio. And I want to be myself," Renata said with finality, pouting a bit.

Renata's sojourn in San Francisco was crowned by the Folederol Ball, held every year for the benefit of the musicians' fund. It is usually given at the Civic Auditorium, but because of the large dimensions of the hall Renata was convinced that it must have been some kind of armory or sport palace.

"It was a very luxurious affair, everything was so beautifully decorated," Renata related. "A small stage was erected in the middle of the hall and all of us who sang at the opera took part in the entertainment. I sang an aria, I don't remember which one. Afterwards we were served dinner at beautifully decorated tables, and then we danced."

Renata likes to dance, but she does so only occasionally, because she likes to choose her own partners. She prefers the slow dances such as the tango, or those which she calls "one step," and she definitely does not like to waltz.

Renata's first partner happened to be a San Francisco lawyer—that much she could gather from the few words they had exchanged. (During her stay in San Francisco Renata's English vocabulary was not much enriched, she still felt safe only with the seven-odd words she had arrived with, and her partner knew no Italian.) Renata has forgotten his name, and as far as she remembers he must have been in his late thirties, rather good-looking, married, and about as tall as Renata. She thinks that he must have had a great deal to drink and that this accounted for his occasionally squeezing her. He did not kiss her, he just squeezed her. On the following day she received a box of flowers with a note apologizing for his behavior. She has never seen or heard from him again.

She retains most pleasant memories of that gay evening except for one thing. She was wearing one of her favorite dresses—"It was like a crinoline made of champagne-colored tulle, volumes of it, with a rather large train," as Renata described it. Unfortunately the dance floor was very crowded; other dancers stepped on her train, and Renata, trying to extricate herself without disturbing her partner's rhythm, often pulled not only the train but what was a rapidly less voluminous skirt. When she returned to her hotel she found that her lovely Milanese gown was in shreds.

Pleased with the success of the performances at the opera and with his latest discovery, Merola took his company to Los Angeles where he presented them at the Shrine Auditorium. Renata enjoyed the train trip along the coast. This was her first real view of any American landscape and she was very much impressed. They were only two weeks in Los Angeles, and although they were busy with rehearsals and performances, still she had at least a glimpse of the movie-land she had heard so much about all her life. With other members of the company she was taken to the Twentieth Century Fox studios where she watched a scene in which Gregory Peck was playing. Later, through Giuseppe di Stefano, the singer, who is an old friend of Danny Kaye, they met the comedian. Renata liked him instantly. "He was so warm, so European," she said. "He kissed us, told us funny stories and made us laugh all the time."

Then they returned to San Francisco, where after parting with the many new friends Renata had made during her short visit, she and Giuseppina took a train to New York, homeward bound. In New York she had only two days before their boat sailed and again she did not see much of the city. But she was happy to be able to see and hear her friends Barbieri and Siepi in Verdi's *Don Carlo* at the Met. Later, backstage, they told her that Toscanini had invited them all for lunch at his home in Riverdale. Next day Walter Toscanini came to pick them up. While they were still in the city, starting on their way, Walter Toscanini called his father over the telephone—Toscanini's luxurious black Cadillac was equipped with one.

"The Maestro was very excited," Renata told me. "He kept asking us how we were, and why we took so long, we were late. 'Hurry up, the lunch is ready, and I am waiting impatiently!' When we arrived at his home, there he was standing at the gate of his garden to welcome us, dressed in his black tunic.

"We were very interested to see his home, which he showed us, as well as his garden. He was very fond of it. One thing particularly stands out in my memory—two enormous bird cages, each with twenty canaries. I understand that he could spend hours sitting close to them, listening."

Of all the musicians Renata has known she holds Toscanini most in awe. Each time she saw him remains a memorable event in her life; every remark he ever made concerning her singing is still in her memory. But Renata did tell me that she thought that Toscanini was very vain. He was well aware of the fact that he was universally considered the best conductor alive. He was pleased that strangers who knew where he lived would drive up to the fence of the garden hoping to catch a glimpse of him. He would sit in the garden or even lean over the fence to let himself be seen. He knew that they were watching him, that they had driven specially, sometimes a long way, to see him—and this pleased him. But if anyone tried to take his picture he would escape into the house.

"The Maestro liked to live in America," Renata said. "It was his home, because he had many friends in the United States, while by that time in Italy he had only a few. Most of his friends in Italy either had died, or were too old, and Maestro loved youth. He was happiest when he was surrounded by young people. Then he was like one of us. We were amazed to see him do everything as if age meant nothing to him. How quickly and easily he would run up and down those stairs in his home if he wanted to fetch something to show us! And he would never let any-one do it for him."

Renata would have liked to stay longer in New York. Although a little tired from all the new impressions and strenuous work in new surroundings she was extremely happy. But she had to go back to Italy where a heavy schedule of performances was awaiting her, bringing with it a difficult new experience.

-- *Chapter 9* --

I do not believe that in the history of music there have
been many interpretive artists who at one time or another
did not suffer from a mishap at one of their performances.
Certainly I do not know of many examples among the
vocalists. Renata Tebaldi seems to have had a very
smooth career ever since Toscanini launched her, but
even she had one "unfortunate incident" of this sort.

In February 1951, Italian musicians commemorated at
La Scala the fiftieth anniversary of Verdi's death. It coin-
cided with the Holy Year—every twenty-five years
Catholics celebrate a Holy Year—during which Victor

de Sabata conducted several performances of sacred music. Renata was engaged to participate in these events. She sang in Bach's *St. Matthew Passion,* in the Mozart and Verdi Requiems, and in other concerts.

Then, on February 3, she gave her first performance of *La Traviata* at La Scala. She had sung the title role of the opera with great success many times before and there was no particular reason for her to worry about it. At the rehearsals everything went well as usual. On the night of the performance, accompanied by her mother, she came to her dressing room and found everything in order. There was nothing to disturb her. Before the beginning of the performance she went into the vocalizing room, and felt she was in good voice.

"At the beginning of the first act I didn't feel anything was wrong," Renata confided to me. "I sang 'E strano, e strano,' and 'Ah! fors è lui,' and I still didn't feel anything wrong with my voice. But when I continued with 'Follie, follie!' and took the high C natural—originally C sharp, which was transposed half a tone lower for me—the high note did not come out as firmly as it should have; it 'wobbled' and the following coloratura passage, because I became nervous, was muffled. I heard a disapproving murmur in the audience, but I continued to sing. As you know, this coloratura passage repeats itself at the end of the aria, and while I was singing it for the second time there was not a sound in the hall."

When the curtain came down and Renata came out to

take her bow, she was greeted with thunderous applause —her admirers threw violets at her feet and she could hear them shout: *"Coraggio, Renata, forza, Renata!"* But this was no help to her. The singer nearly collapsed in her dressing room. She wept and could see that her mother was holding back her tears only to give her daughter the courage to go on.

"I don't remember a single thing of what happened in the following acts. I sang the opera to the end, but I felt as if I were in a coma—I knew nothing of what I was doing. I was like a robot."

After the final curtain she received an ovation, but she was in too much of a daze to understand anything. That night a few of her friends joined the Tebaldis for supper. They tried to distract her, spoke of irrelevant things and managed not to mention what had occurred, but after they left Renata burst into tears again. She cried most of the night. On the following morning she hurried to her doctor, Paolo Vitali-Mazza. He examined her throat and found that her vocal chords were inflamed, that they were "flabby" instead of being tight like a string, and that the right side of her neck was also inflamed. He advised her to take a rest for two months.

"I still had to sing *Aida* but I cancelled the performance and all the other eight scheduled performances of *La Traviata*. This was bad for my reputation, because the announcement of the cancelled performances came out in the papers right after the critic's reviews—they tore me to pieces. If I wanted to prove to them that they were wrong I would have had to sing immediately afterwards, but I simply couldn't."

And indeed, the critics were not so kind to Renata as the audience had been. In his review in the weekly magazine *Oggi* for February 15, 1951, T. Celli wrote that so many "incidents" marred the first performance of *La Traviata* that it seemed as if bad luck was determined to ruin the performance of Verdi's opera. Already in the first act, when the servants were opening the bottles of champagne, corks popped so violently that many of them fell into the orchestra pit. This amused the audience. But the gay atmosphere suddenly changed when Renata Tebaldi was singing her aria.

> The audience, [wrote Signor Celli] grumbled with indignation when Renata Tebaldi completely failed in the top note of the coloratura passage which comes before "Sempre libera degg'io," etc. Although during the dress rehearsal everything went well, at the performance something must have frightened the singer. Besides, Tebaldi's voice is not suited for coloratura and she does not command the high A. Then in the second act, probably still nervous over what had already happened, Tebaldi at first did not sing the right words, but fortunately had the presence of mind to correct the blunder.

According to his report nothing could have saved the performance, for the baritone Giuseppe Taddei also failed to please the audience, and in the third act Gilda Majocchi, the prima ballerina, made her entrance with such impetuosity that she slipped and fell on the floor, which sent the audience into peals of laughter. All this, Celli remarked, must have set the hearts of the singers on the stage to throbbing, for when Tebaldi sang the pathetic "Ah perche venni incauto! Pietà gran Dio di me!" it sounded as if she were bewailing her own choice of singing *La Traviata* before such a demanding audience as that of La Scala.

Nevertheless, [Celli went on] she started the fourth act with extremely clear phrasing and in perfect style and then she sang "Addio del passato" in the most remarkable way. But the devil must have been after her. When she was about to take the high A at the end of the aria something happened to her breath. It caused a slight break in the note, although otherwise she sang it beautifully, clearly and in perfect pitch. These "failings" must have been caused purely by her nervousness, for innumerable times we have heard Tebaldi sing high and long notes with remarkable mastery and beauty. Fear of the La Scala audience? That would have been sufficient. And there should be no shame in admitting it. Didn't Caruso write of "The terrible La Scala in Milan which frightens all artists"?

104

After giving such a complete and detailed account Celli
continued:

> We wish to reaffirm our full confidence and our great
> respect for Renata Tebaldi, because we trust her as one
> of our few singers who "really know how to sing." That
> is to say—she is able to use her beautiful voice with in-
> telligence and perfect style. Her "*note filate,*" her legato
> and her phrasing should be taken as models by every-
> one. But we must admit that she cannot yet be con-
> sidered an "*interprete totale*" because she fails to com-
> bine her great skill of singing with that of acting, as is
> necessary to achieve the complete mastery of a role. She
> obviously plays the part of the "cold" heroine such as
> Desdemona better than the passionate Violetta.

Celli repeated again that in his opinion Tebaldi's vocal
range was not suited for *La Traviata* and he went on to
say that it is a dangerous part and that even the most
famous sopranos with long experience on the stage had
always been obliged to rearrange it in some way. "But
Tebaldi, who is a famous artist, and rightly so, still has too
little experience," he concluded his article. "She should
put Violetta aside, and also she should not sing so much.
The Italian lyric theaters have few singers who are able
to sing as she does, and we want and need her to have a
long career—to be a bright star and not short-lived like
a meteor."

Two other reviews did nothing to soothe Renata's unhappy state of mind. In *L'Europeo* for February 11, 1951, Emilio Radini wrote: "Renata Tebaldi, at present the most beloved soprano of all Italians who love their own music, was evidently not at her ease in the role of Violetta, because of her youth and lack of experience."

And Eugenio Gara said in the daily *Candido:*

It is all right to say that Tebaldi is our most vital and dependable vocal power today. But the personality of Violetta needs to be put in full light with an exceptional mastery and a great skill—something that a young and inexperienced singer like Tebaldi cannot acquire overnight. Besides this, a less pure but more voluptuous voice and a greater "feminine" passion, as Verdi used to call it, are practically essential for an ideal performance of Dumas' heroine. Malibran used to say about Henrietta Sontag, her one rival, "She is very clever, but she has not yet suffered enough. Certain roles you achieve only through your own tears." We do not wish unhappiness to anyone, of course, and of all singers certainly not to our dear Tebaldi, but we are just trying to make ourselves understood. That is all.

"Many people in Milan," Renata continued her sad story, "blamed Victor de Sabata. They said it was he who had let me sing at too many concerts previous to the performance of *La Traviata*. While there may have been a grain of truth in this, I preferred to take on myself the full responsibility for what had occurred. It is true that during the month of January and up to the last days before the performance of *La Traviata* I had a very heavy schedule of rehearsals—almost every day—and four performances a week. Besides, the dress rehearsals for the *St. Matthew Passion* and the Mozart and Verdi Requiems were open to the public, therefore so far as I was concerned they were still extra performances. And all this was going on while I had to rehearse *La Traviata*. But it was not up to Maestro de Sabata. It was up to me. I should have known better."

The incident seems to have aroused such passion among operagoers that within a week two parties were engaged in frenzied arguments for and against de Sabata's art of conducting, which had nothing to do with the case. He was booed during the next performance of *La Traviata* when Lina Aimaro substituted for Renata. The daily papers made an even greater fuss.

Distressed by this attitude, Renata wrote a letter on February 13 to Ghiringhelli in which she expressed her shock over the remarks she had read in the papers and asked him to convey to Maestro de Sabata her admiration and affection for him and her gratitude for everything he had done at La Scala, and her sincere hope of working with him again as soon as she was well. This letter was made public and the incident was soon forgotten. But not by Renata.

"For two months I did nothing except to visit my doctor for treatments. He massaged my throat, poured oil on my vocal chords, gave me some injections for my nerves, but Mamma . . . my poor Mamma, she was so worried. For a whole month she gave me tonic to fortify me. To give *me* more strength!" Renata pointed at her strong arms. She could not help smiling.

But to Giuseppina any illness must have been a vivid reminder of Renata's childhood sufferings with polio, and their aftermath.

I had heard that after this incident Renata had a nervous breakdown and I asked if this was true. "No," Renata shook her head, "it was not so bad as that. But I must confess I was terribly unhappy." At times Renata sincerely believed that she would never be able to sing again. What helped her overcome this nervousness? Perhaps the two months of rest, or possibly the strong Tebaldi religious faith. Mother and daughter could not have been closer during this trying time. But most probably that old remedy for all artistic ailments, an attractive engagement, solved the problem.

It seems that meanwhile in Naples at the San Carlo Opera House they were also commemorating Verdi. Renata has always been even more popular and more admired by the audience at San Carlo than at La Scala. Perhaps just to bolster Renata's spirit, which was at a low ebb, Pasquale Di Contanza, the director of San Carlo, decided to revive Verdi's *Giovanna d'Arco,* which had not been performed for almost a hundred years, especially for Tebaldi.

Renata cannot help laughing whenever she speaks of the opera. "Such a ridiculous libretto—just imagine," she said, "in the second act Giovanna d'Arco has a love duet with the King!"

At the end of her first performance Renata received an ovation. This was important to her. She regained confidence in her voice and after three more performances decided to test herself. She asked Pasquale Di Contanza to let her sing *La Traviata*.

"My friends and my enemies came all the way from Milan to see what was going to happen." This time Renata sang well—indeed so well that she sang *La Traviata* nine times in succession. Baritones and tenors who were her partners in the opera came and went, but for one month and a half, to completely sold-out houses, Renata remained in the title role. She returned the following year for another ten performances.

"And after that, did you go back to La Scala to sing *La Traviata* there?" I asked.

"No, I never did. I sang it over and over again all over Italy and in New York, and I sang in Bergamo, which is very close to Milan, but never at La Scala."

But she never forgot the incident, and I myself have seen that she learned from it a good lesson: to be more careful with her voice.

109

This was shown when in the fall of 1959 Renata went to Vienna to sing at the Staatsoper there during the whole month of September. Despite the fact that she had had a strenuous previous season, followed by six weeks in July and August during which she worked every day on recordings of *Turandot, La Bohème,* and *Tosca,* she was scheduled at the Vienna Opera for several performances of *Aida, Tosca, Otello, Manon Lescaut,* and *Madama Butterfly.* I admired her courage and her discipline, since I knew that she had had only two weeks free before she came to Vienna. I saw her daily in Rome, where the recordings were being made. Rome in the summer is not an Elysium—the temperature hardly ever drops below the eighties; they have little air-conditioning except in two hotels and one American restaurant, and the concert hall of Santa Cecilia, where they were recording, was as hot as a Turkish bath. Although they worked in the evenings, the members of the orchestra vigorously fanned themselves whenever their hands were free, and some of the singers even stripped to the waist. Often because of the unbearable heat the men became irritable, but Renata never complained. Holding a large fan she sat stoically on the stage and would repeat the same aria, or a single passage as often as she was asked to do so by the conductor or the engineers who did the recording. By the end of the second week in August she was exhausted, and yet when we parted in Milan and I suggested that she take a good rest somewhere at the seashore or in the mountains, she said she would rather remain in her apartment in Milan. Thus except for a few drives in the country she had no vacation at all before she went to Vienna.

I remember with what pleasure she was looking forward to these engagements at the Vienna opera. She was very happy that Herbert von Karajan was going to conduct. She knew him and admired him as a musician. But no sooner had she arrived in Vienna than she learned that her program had been changed—she was to have a session recording *Aida* every day and sometimes even twice a day up to the night of her first appearance at the opera, and then would continue to record.

She had been in Vienna only three days when I went to see her in her room at the Hotel Sacher. I found her very depressed. Usually she would have a suite of rooms, but it so happened that the Vienna Trade Fair was taking place at that time and there were literally no rooms to be had because of the thousands of visitors. Renata with her secretary and her dog had to be content with what Sacher could do for her—a room hardly big enough to accommodate all her trunks. But Renata is what is called a good sport and would not complain about something that could not be helped. Nevertheless, the cluttered room must have added to her depression. At first she did not say anything. But she could not keep it to herself and after a bit of coaxing she told me what caused her "misery."

Yes, she said, she was *molto preoccupata*. She meant she was worried.

111

"You remember how happy I was about the prospect of recording the *Aida* with Karajan. I have been looking so much forward to it, and now I wish I had never agreed. Oh why, why did I agree?"

After a while she spoke again. "You see the main trouble here is the atmosphere. It is *troppo pesante*. It is not at all the way it is in Italy, where I always do the recording. You know," she explained, "it is one thing to do a performance and it is another thing to make records. You must have the complete cooperation, almost the close friendship of everyone concerned. And what surprised me was that Karajan, of all conductors, who has been dealing with opera singers for years, does not seem to understand this. Or perhaps he doesn't care," she added after a moment's thought.

"He seems to be interested only in the orchestra and of course first of all in himself. The singers seem to be almost of secondary importance to him. Often some sections, or parts, or even short passages do not come out satisfactorily in the recording, and sometimes simply are bad, and yet he is perfectly content and refuses to do it over again. I understand that where one of Wagner's operas is concerned he is extremely meticulous and will work over and over again striving for perfection. But apparently the Italian operas do not appeal to him as much."

Renata also found his beat rather heavy, not at all elastic, and half the time she could not understand his gestures and indications. In one or two places she thought

112

his beat definitely wrong. She pointed it out to him, but he refused to listen to her. Still, I imagine, with Renata's remarkable discipline and sense of duty she could have put up with it if Karajan had shown some regard for the requirements of Italian singers.

Because the Vienna Philharmonic is busy every night at the opera, the rehearsals for recordings were scheduled for ten o'clock in the morning and the actual recording sessions for three-thirty in the afternoon. But most Italians cannot sing so early in the morning and even three-thirty in the afternoon is still too early for them.

"Do you know at what time I have to get up in the morning?" Renata asked me, as she continued to explain how hard it was physically for her to adjust herself to such a schedule. "At *seven* in the morning, and usually even at ten o'clock I am still asleep, at least my voice is. I simply cannot sing so early in the morning. I am not used to it and I go about yawning all the time. Then at three-thirty it is just as bad, but for another reason. It is too soon after my lunch. My stomach, I suppose, is made that way. It is still digesting and I have no breath left; it is so small it is a catastrophe. *Aida* has a dramatic part, and I have no breath to speak of. I have told all this to Karajan several times, but he doesn't seem to understand. Of course there are some singers who don't mind when they have to sing. There are some who don't need to 'vocalize,' for whom it is sufficient to take a nap after lunch in order to be 'in voice,' as if they were singing in the evening. But I am

113

like most Italian singers, and it is practically impossible for us."

"And what about the matinées you have to sing?" I asked her. "How do you feel about singing as early as two in the afternoon?"

"Ah, that is different. You don't sing matinées every day for two weeks in a row. Once in a while, I imagine, I could sing at any time of day."

Carmen Melis once told me that only the Germans think that a voice is like a violin, that you can play it any time.

Renata further explained how this schedule completely changed her way of living in Vienna. Instead of having her lunch, as she is used to having it in Italy, at one-thirty or two, and her dinner after eight or nine in the evening, she had to have them two hours earlier and go to bed not later than ten in the evening so that she could get up at seven. She said it upset her stomach and her whole well-being.

"Oh, why, why did I agree to do it?" she kept repeating.

I tried to comfort her. "A la guerre comme à la guerre," I reminded her of the old French saying.

"No," she smiled through tears, "in Italian we say 'Once you start dancing at a ball you must keep on.'"

Renata loves to sing; she looks forward to her performances with great pleasure, not at all as if they were hard work. But in Vienna it became an ordeal.

Since Karajan would not change the schedule for the recording sessions, she was faced with the problem of which of the two obligations to fulfill: to record the *Aida* to the end for better or worse, or to carry out her commitment for appearances at the opera. Because so many people were involved in the recording (the singers had come from Italy, and the Decca people from London) she chose to sacrifice her own performance of *Aida* at the opera and was going to cancel *Tosca* also, but the director of the Vienna opera would not let her do it. He told her it was bad enough to cancel *Aida*, and that she could not do the same with *Tosca*, because it had been announced as her first performance with Karajan, and the first performance with the "imported" Italian cast, and the house was sold out on account of it. He insisted that she should keep her engagement. Finally she agreed on condition that beforehand she would be given two days free from recording in order to rest.

By this time Renata looked far from happy. She must have been thinking of all that could happen to her voice if she was overtired. During those two days before the performance of *Tosca*, she hardly even spoke to her secretary. I found her in semi-darkness in her room, listening to records on her portable phonograph. She was listening to Artur Rubinstein playing the Chopin Concerto in F minor, and on the following day she was listening to her friend Siepi's recording of Cole Porter songs. This time she was less depressed and wanted me to explain the title

115

of one of the songs—"I've Got You Under My Skin." I reminded her that she was not to talk. She smiled and with a sad expression said one need not exaggerate, but she would obey if I would do all the talking.

Next day she sang *Tosca* without a single rehearsal. It was a good performance, she was a great success, but it could not be compared to the one she had given at the Metropolitan with Dimitri Mitropoulos conducting. Karajan indeed was much too preoccupied with the orchestra, and on the whole gave the impression that he was afraid of being late for another appointment. Naturally Renata knew that had he given more time and care for the preparation of the work the performance would have benefited by it. "*Ma . . .*" she sighed. She did not need to say another word.

After the performance she went back on her recording schedule. Two days later she realized that she was too exhausted to carry on. This time the old lesson of what happened when she sang *La Traviata* at La Scala stood her in good stead. She was not going to risk it. She canceled the next performance of *Tosca,* and went to see a doctor. As before, her vocal chords were tired and he advised her to rest as much as possible, while he tried some treatments which might still enable her to fulfill the rest of her program at the opera. She managed to finish the *Aida* recording and then again retired to her room. A few days passed, but her voice was not getting any better, and finally the doctor advised her to go back to Milan—a change of air might do her some good, he thought.

This time when I went to see her she was sitting in an armchair next to her phonograph, but she was not listening to records. She was just sitting quietly while her secretary was packing their bags. Renata was very depressed. "When I cannot sing, I just don't feel I am alive," she said.

They were leaving on the first train to Milan. From the occasional remarks they exchanged I gathered that they were especially annoyed at returning to Milan at this time, because Renata had planned to go on a concert tour in Germany right after completing her engagements in Vienna, and now she had to make the extra trip back to Milan. Considering the amount of personal luggage Renata always carries with her, plus two enormous trunks over six feet high containing her stage costumes, and that she had made her decision to leave on short notice, it is easy to imagine the state of the room and of Renata's mind. Yet she did not say a word—never complained of Karajan or the other directors of the opera. It is characteristic of Renata to control anger. Later on, however, she did say to me: "You know, they are strange people— no one, neither Karajan nor the others, has even bothered to call to find out how I was. Not once." It was of no use telling her that it was childish to worry over this. Renata really was hurt by it.

In Milan she remained most of the time in her apartment; sometimes three days would pass without her going out. Her doctor gave her the usual treatment, but after two weeks he advised her to cancel her tour in Germany rather than to worry about it. She had a long winter season before her and she agreed that it would not be worth risking so much.

Thus, I think the "unfortunate incidents" Renata has had in *La Traviata* at La Scala or in Vienna can even be beneficial for a singer who, like her, insists on singing as much as she does.

-- Chapter 10 --

I remember seeing Renata in Paris in the first days of May 1959. We agreed to meet on the Place de L'Opéra after her rehearsal. I still can see her running across the street, waving to me with her handbag—she was a few minutes late. With her long hair blown by the wind and in her beautiful white summer dress it was clear that she could afford to disregard the heavy traffic. Cars jerked and squeaked with the sudden jolt of their brakes and even the policeman with his uplifted white baton turned around and stared at her. But he said nothing. Would a

Frenchman say anything to a beautiful young woman for breaking the traffic laws?

"This is not Milan, you'll get hurt," I told her as I led her through the throng on the Boulevard des Capucines. "Don't you know Paris at all?" I asked.

"No, not much . . ." she said, looking eagerly over the heads of the crowd into the windows of the stores we were passing. "I have been here only once before and then only about ten days or so."

That was during the spring of 1951, soon after her performances in *La Traviata* in Naples. The San Carlo Opera company was invited to come to Paris. It was the first time since World War II that a foreign organization came to the French capital. The Italians gave four performances, two each of *Giovanna d'Arco*, and *Un Ballo in Maschera*. They brought with them their own scenery, the complete staff of the company, and the orchestra. Gabriele Santini conducted.

"The French loved *Giovanna d'Arco*," Renata told me later, and from the way her eyes sparkled I knew that she was still thinking of that love duet in the second act between Jeanne d'Arc and the King, which always amuses her.

"Ah, there is La Madeleine," Renata pointed it out to me as she recognized the church. "I sang there in Verdi's *Requiem*. We gave one performance . . . But where are we?" she asked and only when we reached the Place de

la Concorde did she remember that she had been there
before.

I took Renata to Chez Weber on rue Royale because
I had promised to show her the café where at one time
literati, the painters, musicians and even politicians used
to gather in groups at tables specially reserved for them.
I told her about some of them who would inevitably in
late afternoon or evening pass through the doors of Chez
Weber. Pierre Louÿs, the author of *Aphrodite,* always
very elegantly dressed, was one, and another was Oscar
Wilde, who would order a drink for himself and also a
glass and a bottle of Vichy water to refresh the sunflower
which he carried in his hand. Marcel Proust used to come
in sometimes at about seven in the evening, gravely an-
nouncing that he had just got up, that he had a cold and
a headache, that the noise made him sick and he was going back to bed. But he often stayed until the early hours
of the morning. Claude Debussy strolled in after dinner.
He sat by himself reading his newspaper, oblivious to
the conversations around him.

Renata loved these stories, she would sit and listen to
every word paying no attention to whatever was happening around her—waiters carrying their trays, young
couples discussing their plans for the evening as they
passed our table. Renata has a remarkable memory.
Often she will surprise me with a wealth of minor details in connection with one of my own stories. When

I ask, "How do you know all this?" she replies, "You must have forgotten you told me that once." And then she quotes me verbatim. I presume it is her excellent ear and musical memory. Just as she can sing from memory, and in perfect pitch, a whole page out of a composition I have played for her, but which she had never heard before.

But on this occasion she was more interested in my story about the decision that was taken one night in Chez Weber—which of the two sopranos, Mary Garden or Georgette Leblanc, was to sing the title role at the première of Debussy's *Pelléas et Mélisande,* a decision which almost led the poet Maurice Maeterlinck, Leblanc's husband, to challenge Albert Carré, then the director of the Opéra-Comique, to a duel.

"So rivalries among us, the opera singers, are an old story, aren't they?" Renata said, and I felt that on this beautiful spring day in Paris she would much rather talk about something else, about all the amusement places, theaters, cabarets, nightclubs, and of course the dressmaking establishments which intrigue every woman who comes to Paris.

She told me that during her short previous visit she did not have a chance to see as much of Paris as she would have liked to. She had been in the Louvre, and she remembered several historical monuments and places. But she had also seen a little of the lighter part of Paris, which she enjoyed very much. Chaperoned by

Giuseppina she went to the Folies Bergères, the Lido night club, and the Tabarin, but she missed going to the Moulin Rouge. Somehow as she spoke about it I felt that Renata thought of Paris as a "naughty" town. This may be the reason she thinks of the Parisians as superficial people.

"But of course I love Paris," she repeated several times. And yet she has never cared for Parisian *haute couture*. She has never bought a single dress in Paris. She thinks that Parisian styles are much too complicated, at least for her. She prefers the more simple—the Italian style of her own dressmaker Rosita Contreras, who has an establishment in Milan and one in Rome.

"And what about Mamma, didn't she like the Parisian styles?" I asked.

"Mamma was very difficult—she never cared for clothes as I do. All her life she was very modest, and I couldn't do anything with her. She said she didn't care whether she looked elegant or not. It would take many hours of arguments before I would succeed in making her agree that a new nice coat or a dress was very becoming to her. And then she would insist that if she did get it, it would be the last one. Of course I agreed until the next time. I was always convinced that whenever she bought a new dress, or a fur piece, it was only because she wanted to please me. It was the same with the few pieces of jewelry she had. But she loved to go window-shopping with me."

123

"Is that a hobby of yours?" I asked.

"Not a hobby, it is my passion."

But Renata is not satisfied with window-shopping only. Twice a year she visits the Italian couturiers to see their summer and winter collections and she admits that sometimes she spends as much as two to three hours watching them and has "the most marvelous time." She told me that she loves furs, fine lingerie, beautiful nightgowns, and every type of jewelry—from diamonds to the most simple trinkets if they are beautiful: earrings, bracelets, necklaces and rings. "In fact," she said, "I love everything that every other woman does."

On stage and off Renata has an enormous wardrobe and she changes her clothes constantly. She is never certain of her choice and is always pleased when complimented. But she is very suspicious of compliments and insists that she can always tell if it is done just *pro forma,* just to be polite.

She said she had developed this taste for finery when she began to sing in public and saw for the first time the "elegant" world. From then on nothing else gave her so great a pleasure. She buys about fifty dresses a year. "That is not too much," she tried to explain, "you forget there are four seasons in a year." But all her stage costumes are made at La Scala. Only one is an exception— her present gown for the second act of *Tosca* was made at the Vienna Opera House.

In winter she wears hats. But she says that as she is

124

very fickle in everything she soon gets tired of them. While she keeps on giving some of them to her friends and relatives, she thinks that she usually has in her closets at least two hundred of them. Often she will walk into a store and buy as many as ten hats. It has happened that she would buy some hats just because she saw them in the window display. Later, when she tried them at home, she found she did not like them and would leave them locked up in her closets. This kind of waste used to annoy her mother, who otherwise did not mind her extravagance. The same thing still happens with her shoes and handbags. She has dozens and dozens of them, yet she keeps buying new ones.

Recently she has been very much preoccupied with her new coiffure. She changes it almost every day, because she cannot remember which way it suits her best, and like a child she always asked me whether it was better or less becoming than it had been on the previous day. If I said that I had forgotten some small detail which seemed to her to make a great difference, she would look disappointed, almost peeved. Pouting, she would insist that I should help her to recapture the lost effect. She says that the arrangement of her hair depends entirely on her mood and sometimes it just does not come out right.

I asked her if there was anything in particular that she would like to have, anything that she had been "daydreaming" about. Without any hesitation she said "No."

She has everything. She does not want to have a car of her own, because this would mean that she would have to have a regular driver, and nothing makes her more nervous than to be conscious of someone sitting and waiting for her while she is on one of her shopping tours. She prefers to hire a car whenever she needs one. Renata has learned to drive a car herself and has a license, but she would not care to drive any great distance, even from Milan to Rome. It is much too far and tiring, she says.

She also does not like to have many servants. One or two are perfectly sufficient for her, because she does not like to be bothered by many people around her. In Milan where she has her only real home, Consolata, who has been with her since 1952, keeps her apartment spotlessly clean. Consolata is a dignified and good-looking woman in her late fifties who loves music. However, Consolata is set in her ways and some of them irritate Renata: Renata prefers to leave a large antique secretary in her living room open, showing a beautiful collection of crystal and porcelain. But Consolata apparently does not approve, and she carefully closes the doors of the cupboard each time Renata leaves them open. And she can be extremely difficult about certain dishes when Renata decides to have one for dinner on the spur of the moment. It is as if she had to have longer notice for the proper inspiration she requires.

Renata's apartment is beautifully situated in the quiet Sito-Guastalla section within walking distance of the

Cathedral and La Scala. But Renata feels that once the furnishing is completed she would like to move somewhere else. Contrary to what has always been said about it, her apartment is far from large, but comfortable and perfectly sufficient for her. The only good-sized room is her sitting room which somehow gives a Venetian impression, probably because Renata prefers bare floors. There are no rugs in the small entrance hall which leads to the sitting room, or in the room itself. There on her small grand piano—a Steinway which she bought in 1952 before it could be displayed at an exhibition in Milan—she has inscribed photographs of Toscanini and Mitropoulos. Her dining room is intimate—I doubt that she could seat more than six guests—and besides her own bedroom she has two small guest rooms. And that is all. This is Renata's choice and she would not want anything larger.

·· Chapter 11 ··

In the spring of 1951, the year of Renata's first trip to Paris, after having heard Renata in *Otello, Tosca,* and *La Traviata,* Barretto Pinto, a concert manager from Rio de Janeiro, engaged her, along with several other singers from La Scala, for the following season at the opera house in Rio.

On August 12 of that year Renata drove with her mother from Milan to Genoa where they boarded the *Conte Grande.* From what I have gathered it appears that this particular group of singers did not travel like members of one happy family. Some of them went earlier, others later. Antonio Votto, who was to conduct the performances, went by himself, and Maria Callas, another member of the company, took a plane with her husband. Although on board Renata found several of her good friends, such as the tenor Gianni Poggi, Boris Christoff, and Mario del Monaco with their wives, and also Fedora Barbieri and Elena Nikolai, the twelve days voyage did not bring them any closer.

Renata is not quite certain whether it is a characteristic trait of all performing artists, but she thinks that, speaking generally, opera singers are a narrow-minded, mean, selfish and gossipy lot. Some of them suffer, she says, from having a too *superbo* notion of themselves, others would like to be taken for intellectuals, and there are still others among them who claim higher social standards, a more impressive background and even an aristocratic heritage, and behave like silly snobs. Such superior attitudes bore Renata and at times irritate her.

When they get together, as she says, they like to "rip everyone apart" (those who are not present, of course) and somehow Renata has never enjoyed this particular sport. She preferred then usually to remain alone with her mother. She developed this aloofness, as some who condemn her call it, almost from the beginning of her operatic career. She has always been against profane language and vulgarity. She felt that backstage some men seem to behave as if they were by themselves in a

bar, and even took a sadistic pleasure in shocking innocent girls like herself. They told her risqué jokes which
usually went over her head, then took a great delight in
explaining them and "educating" her.

As she always tried to keep a certain distance from
her colleagues, she saw no reason just because she happened to be in closer quarters with them during this
voyage to alter her attitude. Besides, she said, each of
them followed his own habits, so they were not forced
to see each other all the time—some took their meals
earlier than others, some took naps, while others prome-
naded on deck or played cards.

Despite the perfect weather Renata was not alto-
gether happy about this, her first crossing of the ocean
by ship. Neither she nor her mother were good sailors.
And she admits that since there was no reason for her
not to feel well, it must have been due to pure nervousness—perhaps an anticipation of something unpleasant.
She spent most of her days lying in a deck chair, until
one of the officers convinced her that a bit of exercise on
a dummy bicycle would do her good.

Renata never did get used to the sea, although she
has made a great many trips across the ocean since. She
hardly dares to eat or drink, despite everyone's advice,
and she suffers in silence. She used to be afraid of flying
and would take a plane only if there were no other way,
but during the past two seasons, no doubt influenced by
the example of her friends, she has been flying across

the ocean, and now she tells me that she really enjoys it.

For their work the singers were given a room with an upright piano and there Renata did her daily vocalizing, and worked on her part in *La Traviata* with Gino del Signore, a tenor who played the piano well and could accompany her.

Renata had heard so much about the beauty of the Rio harbor that as they approached it she got up at five in the morning to see it. But the mist marred the picture. However, she has seen it since, and thinks it beautiful, although she prefers the view of Naples. In Rio they were housed in a beautiful hotel, and from her room she could see the Sugar Loaf and the whole panorama of Guanabara Bay.

They arrived three days before the opening night. Being in a country which knew nothing of the privations due to the last war, Renata wanted to buy every beautiful shawl, materials for dresses and all sorts of souvenirs, and probably would have brought back home suitcases full of what she saw on her window-shopping tours had the rehearsals not started almost immediately after their arrival, leaving her little time for anything else. The Italian company opened the season with *La Traviata* with Renata in the title role. It was a great success, and later she was heard in *La Bohème* and *Aida*.

It was there, in Rio, that the much publicized "feud" between Maria Callas and Renata Tebaldi began. Renata is very reticent about it. In all the time I have known her she would never mention Maria Callas' name to me, unless I happened to see her soon after one of Madame Callas' remarks to the press against Renata, and then only if I brought the subject up. It would be naive to think that she feels friendly toward Madame Callas, but her resentment is based entirely on Madame Callas' uncalled-for "observations" about Renata's personal life. Renata says that there should never have been any "feud" between two such sopranos, even if in the eyes of some people they were bound to be rivals. It is the press, she says, who wish to make a sensation out of something that is not uncommon in the theater. "In Italy," she said, "they love to watch rivalry among artists. Just think of Malibran and Sontag or Patti and Christine Nilsson."

"And why speak of hatred when there never has been any love between us, and why speak of enemies if we have never been friends?" Renata asks.

Nevertheless, Renata does seem to feel strongly about Madame Callas. But she feels she is in a far better position if she controls her temper when attacked by her adversary, and by her dignified attitude she has gained sympathy and admiration, while Madame Callas continues to attract attention with any new outburst. I refer to Madame Callas' statement in *Time* on November 3, 1958:

My admiration of her is of the fullest, and I am happy for her success. If I hear her sing well, I am the first to

132

cheer her. But I live in another world. She is a vocalist of a certain repertoire. I consider myself a soprano—one who does what they used to do once upon a time. My repertoire, by God's will and nature's blessing, is complete. I have contributed to the history of music. I have taken music that has long been dead and buried and have brought it back to life again. If the time comes when my dear friend Renata Tebaldi will sing, among others, *Norma* or *Lucia* or *Anna Bolena* one night, then *La Traviata* or *Gioconda* or *Medea* the next—then, and only then, will we be rivals.

Renata's repertoire consists of thirty-six operas—an adequate number for one lifetime. As for Madame Callas' "living in another world," she has never spoken a truer word. During the months of July and August, 1959, the newspapers on both continents gave a full report of it.

Madame Callas closes her account of the accomplishments of Maria Callas with: "Otherwise it is like comparing champagne with cognac. No—champagne with Coca-Cola." And she added to the same *Time* reporter: "What I really wish for her is that she find some wonderful person to marry. Love completes a woman; her art would be even better."

In the same reports about "her world," everyone read about Madame Callas' "love," but what improvement it made in her art still remains to be seen, for today many large opera houses on both continents appear to be closed to her.

133

In an article in several installments in the Italian magazine *Oggi* Madame Callas wrote about herself and of course gave a detailed account of her relationship with Renata Tebaldi. I find Madame Callas' self-portrait so well drawn that I prefer to refrain from any touching up of the picture, and will just set straight some of the facts concerning her relationship with Renata Tebaldi, which must have become obscure in the memory of Madame Callas, most probably because of the many years that have elapsed since the events took place: she wrote in 1957 about things which had happened in 1947 and 1951.

In the first article entitled "La Mia Cara Amica Tebaldi," she said: "I believe that seldom between two women of the same age and the same profession can there be a *simpatia* as fresh and spontaneous as that which occurred between us." This according to Madame Callas happened in Venice.

Actually Renata met Madame Callas for the first time in Verona in 1947 where, during the summer Festival, Madame Callas was singing in Amilcare Ponchielli's *La Gioconda*. They were both at a party at Castello Romano, but except for a few polite words when they were introduced they said nothing to each other. In those days Madame Callas weighed close to two hundred pounds, was careless of her personal appearance, and was less than perfectly groomed. As I have already noted several times, personal appearance influences Renata's reaction

134

—thus there could not have been any love at first sight, at least on Renata's part.

Later they did meet again in Venice. Here is what Madame Callas wrote about it in the same article:

> One night during the performance of *Tristan*, while I was making up in my dressing room, I heard the door open unexpectedly, and in the doorway stood the tall figure of Tebaldi, who was in Venice to sing—I don't know whether for the first time—*Traviata* with Serafin. We knew one another only by sight, but on this occasion we shook hands warmly and Renata addressed such spontaneous compliments to me that I was enchanted. I remember that I was particularly impressed by a phrase, that I, a foreigner, and one who had spent little time in Italy, had never heard. "*Mamma mia,*" she said to me, "if I had been obliged to go through such a tiring role, they would have had to scoop me up with a spoon."

What actually happened was less dramatic but more characteristic of Madame Callas. By that time (that is, when they met in Venice) Madame Callas was already married to Giovanni Battista Meneghini, the wealthy Veronese industrialist. Meneghini undertook to make an opera star out of his bride by first streamlining her figure, and then by paying large sums for her long and serious studies with Tullio Serafin. Meneghini happened to be in Madame Callas' dressing room when *after* the per-

135

formance Renata came to see her. It is unlikely that if
Renata went to congratulate her she would say anything
unpleasant. But what Renata distinctly remembers was
that no sooner had she finished complimenting her on
her performance than Madame Callas, presenting Meneghini to her, said: "I wish you too would have such a
wonderful husband."

> My *simpatia* for her became real affection a short time
> later in Rovigo, [Madame Callas continued her story]
> where Tebaldi was singing in *Andrea Chenier* and I was
> singing *Aida*. At the end of the aria "O cieli azzurri" I
> heard a voice shout from one of the boxes, *"Brava, brava
> Maria!"* It was the voice of Renata. From then on, we
> became—I can well say it—dearest friends. We were
> often together; we exchanged advice on dress, coiffure,
> and even on repertoires. Afterwards, however, our pro-
> fessional commitments did not permit us to fully enjoy
> this friendship: we met briefly, between one voyage or
> another, but always I think, or rather I feel sure, with
> reciprocal pleasure. She admired me for my dramatic
> strength and my physical endurance, and I admired her
> *dolcissimo canto*.

Renata did hear Madame Callas in *Aida* in Rovigo,
and it is true—it was Renata's voice Madame Callas
heard shouting *"Brava, brava Maria!"* This only shows
Renata's fairness toward her colleague's performance,
but it had nothing to do with Renata's attitude toward

Madame Callas as a person. As a matter of fact Renata was not enthusiastic enough to go backstage to congratulate her after the performance as she had before in Venice. Actually the two divas never spoke to each other at any length until they were in Rio de Janeiro. So all the talk about their great friendship and their often being together, "discussing their dress, coiffure, and even their repertoires" is a pure fantasy of Madame Callas, Renata says.

Of their meeting in Rio Madame Callas said, in the next installment of the article:

Actually, it was in Rio that the first collision occured between Renata and me. We had not seen one another in a long time and we were happy to meet again. I, at least, was sincerely happy. I remember that we were always together in the gay restaurants of Rio: I, she, her mother, Battista [Meneghini] and Elena Nikolai and her husband. Then, one fine day, Signor Barretto Pinto —a rather simple man, but one who is quite powerful in financial and political circles, and who is married to one of the richest women in Brazil—asked the singers to take part in a benefit concert. We didn't know—I still don't know—for the benefit of what organization this concert was given, nevertheless we accepted and Renata proposed and we all agreed not to sing any encores. But when her turn came, she silenced the applause given her for her singing of the "Ave Maria" from *Otello*, and began, to our great surprise, a "Romanza" from

137

Andrea Chenier, and right after that, she sang "Vissi d'arte" from *Tosca.* I felt badly about it. I had prepared only my special piece "Sempre libera" from *Traviata,* but I gave to this gesture of Renata's only the importance that one would give to the caprice of a child. Only later, during the dinner that followed the concert did I realize that my dear colleague and friend had changed in her attitude toward me, and that she could not hide a touch of bitterness every time she addressed me.

All of this, to be sure, is unimportant, but I was upset. We were dining at a round table—and with us was Nikolai. Renata Tebaldi began to speak of her unsuccessful attempt at *Traviata* at La Scala, making me aware of the difficulties that I too had come up against during my appearance in Milan. I answered rather sharply and remember that Titta [Battista Meneghini] nudged me with his elbow several times to cut short the discussion. Everything would have ended there with that brisk exchange of words, if it hadn't been for the incident of *Tosca.*

In Madame Callas' article this is the first critical and jealous expression of her feeling toward Renata. Everything would indeed "have ended there," had not the Rio opera by chance offered a sort of arena for competition by two operatic gladiators—they both sang in the same operas and even appeared on the same concert program. Incidentally, it was a benefit performance for the Red Cross. Everyone knew about it, except, it seems, Madame Callas. Renata never did propose "not to sing any encores." All the singers knew that at such a performance they were expected to give encores. Madame Callas does not like to sing encores. But she insisted on being the last performer before the first intermission—a very important place for a performer, for the public's applause can be taken as being for that particular artist rather than including all the other singers who participated in the first part of the program.

Renata would not have minded the division in the audience's preference—this was part of the game—but she did mind Madame Callas choosing to sing at that concert the aria from *La Traviata,* with which Renata had by then made a great impression in Rio. But these, I agree with Madame Callas, were mere pinpricks, and would have never caused serious trouble between them, as she said, if it were not for the "incident" of *Tosca.*

Here, however, I must interrupt Madame Callas' narrative before she speaks of the incident in order to set straight the chronological sequence of the events.

It was not at the dinner after the concert, but long before that benefit performance, that one fine day Madame Callas and Elena Nikolai with their husbands, and Renata with her mother, happened to be sitting at the same round table in the restaurant having lunch. As they were discussing various performances, it was Madame Callas and not Renata who brought up the subject of Renata's first performance of *La Traviata* at La Scala.

139

(I take it for granted that my reader, by now well informed about the whole story of Renata's performance in *La Traviata,* would find it highly unlikely that Renata would mention it.) This was a painful reminder to Renata, for whom, according to general knowledge, it was the first and only really unfortunate incident in her career. Naturally she did not care to discuss it with Madame Callas. But Madame Callas persisted, offering her all sorts of advice—among other things she said that Renata should not sing so many operas at La Scala. "This," she said, "is not good either for you or for the audience." (Madame Callas must have changed her mind when she spoke to the reporter from *Time* magazine, whom I have mentioned before.) She talked so much about it that it seemed to turn into a lecture.

"She herself then was singing all the time, as many as forty performances in a season," Renata said to me, "and I didn't see why she should be telling me all this. Although I said nothing, Meneghini apparently realized that she had already said more than was wise, for he must have pressed her foot under the table signaling her to stop."

"You didn't see him do it, did you?" I asked Renata.

"No, I didn't. But both Mamma and I were convinced of it, for Callas suddenly turned in a perfect rage against her husband shouting: 'Leave me alone, you are *stupido,* you don't know and don't understand anything in these matters. Leave me alone, do you hear me? And don't you dare to interrupt me!' Meneghini never did say a word, not during her monologue, nor after."

And now I shall let Madame Callas continue her story.

After the benefit concert in Rio de Janeiro, Renata Tebaldi left for São Paulo, where she was to sing in *Andrea Chenier*. I stayed in Rio for the first performance of *Tosca*. The discussions between me and my colleague had not been allowed to trail on; our relationship remained cordial, if a little less affectionate. But during my performance of *Tosca* a disturbing incident occurred. I had just finished the aria of the second act when through the applause I clearly heard someone shout the name of another singer, Elisabetta Barbato, and start up dissenters in one section of the audience. I succeeded in controlling myself, in not letting depression and panic defeat me, and at the end of the opera, I was rewarded by a long and warm ovation. Nonetheless, the following day, the director of the Teatro dell' Opera, Senhor Barretto Pinto of whom I have already spoken, called me to his office, and without further ado, told me that I was not to sing any more on subscription evenings. In other words, I was *protestata*, as they say in theatrical slang.

At first surprise made me unable to speak, but afterwards (unjust accusations always make me rebel) I reacted hotly. I shouted that my contract stated that in addition to *Tosca* and *Gioconda*—operas given only to subscribers—there would be two non-subscription performances of *Traviata*, and that they had to pay me for

141

them, if they prevented me from singing. Barretto got mad. "All right," he said—he had no choice—"sing *Traviata,* but I warn you now that no one will come to hear you." He proved to be a bad prophet because every seat in the theater was taken for both performances. Nevertheless, he didn't give up, and tried to annoy me in other ways. I remember well that when I went to get my pay he turned to me and spoke these exact words: "For the performance you gave I shouldn't pay you anything." I was seized with a blind rage and grabbed the first object I could find on his desk to hurl it at his head, and if someone hadn't taken me by the arm, I don't know what would have happened.

It is easy to guess what would have happened. Presuming that Madame Callas' markmanship was not as good as that of William Tell, and that Senhor Pinto had sufficient sense of humor and presence of mind to lay her across his knee and give her a sound spanking, I believe he might have rendered her a good service and Madame Callas might have learned more appropriate behavior for the office of the director of an opera house. Then the closed doors of many opera houses on both continents would perhaps still be open to her.

But to return to her version of what happened with *Tosca,* and Renata's part in it.

I have recounted this unpleasant episode of my career, [Madame Callas refers to the one with Senhor Pinto] because it was tied to another bitterness. As I have said, while I was singing *Tosca* in Rio, Renata was singing in *Andrea Chenier* in São Paulo. Naturally, having been *protestata*—and in such a manner—I was curious to learn the name of the soprano who was to replace me in *Tosca*. And I learned, to my sorrow, that they were speaking of Renata, the singer I had always considered my best friend, rather than just a colleague. They said that Tebaldi had ordered a copy of the costumes that I had tried on for *Tosca*, and gone to the dressmaker who had made them for me; not only that, but she had gone to try them on before leaving for São Paulo, that is, when no one could have predicted or known that I would be *protestata*.

This insinuation of a plot presumably concocted by Senhor Pinto and Renata hardly deserves a comment. Obviously Madame Callas became a bit emotional after she was booed at her *Tosca* performance and because of her *contretemps* with Senhor Pinto. It is understandable that in her state of mind she saw devils pursuing her. But Renata was not one of them. As Madame Callas correctly stated, Renata was in São Paulo. Two days after Madame Callas' performance Renata received a telephone call from Senhor Pinto asking her if she would return to Rio to sing the next performance of *Tosca*. Renata did and had a great success. As for Madame Callas' story about Renata ordering copies of her costumes, it is misinformation, as Renata was not scheduled to sing

Tosca in Rio—it was not in her contract. Therefore there was no question of her ordering costumes before she went to São Paulo. She never expected to be asked to sing *Tosca,* and the costumes in which she finally appeared had to be made within twenty-four hours, when she returned from São Paulo. "You should have seen them, you cannot imagine what they looked like," Renata told me.

As I have said Renata had a great success with her performance of Floria Tosca. Madame Callas by then was already back in Europe, but she heard about it. She never forgave Renata, and this started the "feud."

When Renata returned to Milan she soon discovered that the audiences were divided into two almost warring groups of admirers—hers and those of Callas. They were nicknamed Tebaldiani and Callasiani, like the Gluckists and Piccinists of the eighteenth century. And at every performance they passionately expressed their preference by loud boos or bravos. Whether it is true or not I do not know, but many Milanese were under the impression that there was a claque which had a double assignment—to create ovations for Maria Callas, and to boo Tebaldi. But Madame Callas must have failed to win the Milanese completely. As late as the summer of 1959, a friend of mine happened to be eating spaghetti in one of the restaurants near La Scala. She bit on a nail, and called the waiter to show him her discovery. The waiter apologized: "They must have taken you for Madame Callas," he said.

While Renata was singing at La Scala, Madame Callas used to come to every rehearsal and every performance and sit in the director's box, which is right above one side of the stage, and carefully watch every step, every movement Renata made. To see those big black eyes "trying to hypnotize her" made Renata nervous. Eventually the antics of Madame Callas succeeded in making Renata so uncomfortable that her mere presence in the theater was unbearable.

However I think it is only fair to let Madame Callas give her own interpretation of the facts:

> I should like to say that if I followed her performances with attention, I did so only to discover in every detail how Renata sings; and I am infinitely sorry to hear the ridiculous accusation flung at me that I went to "intimidate" her. The public, Renata, and even more, the people with whom she surrounds herself, cannot understand that I—and I am not ashamed of it—shall always find something to learn in the voices of all my colleagues, not only the famous ones like Tebaldi, but also the humble and mediocre ones. Even the voice of a very modest pupil can serve as a lesson. And I who have tortured myself hour after hour in search of continuous improvement shall never give up listening to the singing of my colleagues.

145

Let the reader draw his own conclusion from this mealy-mouthed statement. But I would like to quote the last paragraph written by Madame Callas on this subject:

> Even now [1957] every time I think of this episode [*Tosca* in Rio] which now belongs to the past, I tell myself that Renata could not have meant to ruin our good friendship, and that perhaps there was a misunderstanding, painful and incomprehensible, at the root of all this. And if circumstances may appear to be unfavorable to her and to those who surround her, I try to convince myself that between us, there is nothing more than a misunderstanding, and I shall continue to hope sincerely that it will be resolved some day.

Madame Callas wrote this while she reigned supreme at La Scala, and I presume that it was only to foster her sincere hope of resolving the misunderstanding between herself and Renata that a year later she made her remark about Coca-Cola to the reporter of *Time* magazine. I have tried to present the whole story impartially, but I cannot help but feel that if Madame Callas would do more singing and less talking she would resolve more than one of her problems. And I sincerely hope that somebody will explain to her the difference between "fame" and "notoriety."

Despite her feelings Renata tries to be fair and give La Callas her due. Like some musicians in Italy, including Carmen Melis, Renata thinks that Maria Callas has a voice, well trained, but not great, with three different ranges. This in itself is remarkable.

Renata says that Madame Callas in life is not a beautiful woman, but on the stage she often appears beautiful. But what amazes her most is that Maria Callas, who is so short-sighted that she can barely see anything at all without glasses and often has to squint, runs up and down the stage over so many steps as she does in *Medea* without any difficulty whatsoever.

Renata says that she admires her perseverance. "She seems to succeed in everything she desires. She wanted money—she married a rich man. She wanted clothes and jewelry—she has them now. She wanted to become thin, and she did. She wanted La Scala, and she succeeded." And yet as Renata said this to me I could easily see in her attitude more pity for Madame Callas than envy.

Eventually for several years Madame Callas managed to be the star at La Scala. She was treated as such by the management of the opera and she was given her choice of the best operas in the repertoire. This Renata felt was unfair, unfair to the other singers as well as to herself. "I decided to leave La Scala," Renata told me. "It was very hard for me, for I have always considered myself La Scala's own creation. But . . . unfortunately I had no other choice," Renata added in a low voice, as if she were speaking of parting forever with her beloved. It was even more than that. Renata had had to admit a defeat. It was humiliating, particularly to one as proud as she.

During the following years the management of La Scala often wrote her asking Renata to change her mind and to return. "But I was stubborn," Renata said firmly, "and I refused to return so long as Maria Callas reigned there."

-- Chapter 12 --

Renata is firmly convinced that an artist's career chiefly depends on his "wisdom." He should never rest on his laurels, never slack in the constant improvement of his work, paying the most meticulous attention to every detail. It should be done without haste, patiently. So far she has never accepted an offer to sing something that was new to her until she was completely confident of her ability to do her absolute best. This sometimes meant that she would have to wait a long time, or perhaps even never have another opportunity of performing the offered work. But this she does not regret. "With a clear conscience I can say," she once told me, "that I have never done anything 'too soon' in my life." And this was one of the reasons why it took her so many years before she made her debut in New York.

Two opera houses bestow the final recognition of their art upon singers from all over the world: La Scala in Milan and the Metropolitan Opera House in New York. Like other artists who were acclaimed at La Scala, Renata expected that sooner or later she too would have to pass this test, but faithful to her own dictum she was willing to bide her time before appearing at the American Parnassus.

Shortly after her initial success in Italy, after Toscanini had launched her, Edward Johnson, then the director of the Metropolitan, heard her and when he saw her in Milan in 1948 he offered her a contract. Renata felt it was much too early for her—she was not ready. "I was but a young chicken," she says, and she declined. Later, Rudolf Bing, the present manager of the Metropolitan, asked her, as he did Cesare Siepi and several other La Scala singers, to audition for him. This, all of them, including Renata, refused to do. "We were no longer beginners and we didn't need to audition any more. If Mr. Bing wanted to, he could have heard us at one of the performances."

Another year or two elapsed, and Rudolf Bing heard Renata in *Aida* in San Francisco. He came back stage to

Parimage, Calzolari, Paris

Paris—1958

Falstaff,
with Victor de Sabata
—1950

Publifoto, Milan

Giovanna d'Arco (Verdi)
in Naples—1951

Troncone, Naples

As Violetta—1957

Louis Mélançon, New York

Troncone, Naples

With Miriam Pirazzini
in *Adriana Lecouvreur*
(Cilea)—1958

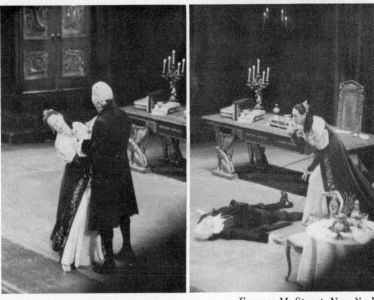

Act Two of *Tosca*, with George London —1959

Traviata at the Met

Louis Mélançon, New York

With Aoyama, rehearsing for
Butterfly—1959

Louis Mélançon, New York

Butterfly's death—1959

Mark Hagmann, Philadelphia

Manon Lescaut at the Met—1959

Farabola, Milan

Triumph at La Scala, with Di Stefano
and Maestro Gavazzeni—1959

Farabola, Milan

After the performance at La Scala—1959

Renata with Tina—1959

Renata relaxes—1959

congratulate her and this time he offered her a "tryout"
at the Met. He suggested that on her way home to Italy
she should do two performances of Donna Elvira in Mozart's *Don Giovanni* and one of *La Bohème*. Renata refused again: "I didn't feel like singing once or twice in
New York. Either I was going to be engaged for a whole
season, or I would have to wait until the management of
the Met had more confidence in me." During the following three years she heard nothing from Mr. Bing; then in
the spring of 1954 he came for his annual visit to Milan
and then he offered her a contract for the second part of
the following season, that of 1954–1955.

I saw Renata shortly after she arrived with her mother
on the *Andrea Doria* in New York, to be exact three days
before her debut. In those days Renata had no secretary.
She did not need one. Giovanni Careno, a young Venetian, who is now in the diplomatic service, an old friend of
the family, served her as interpreter. As we sat in her
apartment at the Buckingham Hotel on 57th Street we
spoke of those days, long gone by, when we had first met
in Milan, and I had predicted in my reports to the American magazines that when she came to New York she
would be a sensational success. Almost nine years had
passed, during which she had been singing to sold-out
houses in Italy, in Paris, in London, in San Francisco, and
in Rio de Janeiro, but she neither behaved nor looked like
a great prima donna. She still looked like a very young
girl. Only now she had a different coiffure. She brushed

her hair straight back from her forehead, which gave her even more the appearance of a college girl. She wore a wide dark blue skirt and a sweater over a shirt as simple as a man's, with the collar open and the cuffs turned back over pushed-up sleeves. She kept sliding a small ring up and down her finger—she did not need to tell me that she was very nervous.

Was it her part in *Otello* which made her nervous? I asked.

"No, no, this time it is different. It is not the opera; it's waiting all these days before the performance. I wish it were tonight so it would all be over," she sighed. And indeed she gave the impression of a student who has learned all he can about a subject and is impatient to get on with the examination—for better or worse, to pass or to fail.

To distract her I asked her about her impressions of New York. But she confessed that her mind was much too preoccupied with the coming event for her to enjoy any sightseeing. Both she and her mother were bewildered by the city. "It is so big," she said. "It seems much the largest city I have ever been to. Mamma definitely doesn't like New York. It frightens her. She feels lost, so far from her relatives and friends. So far from home, from Langhirano." Renata thought for a while. "But I like New York," she continued, "It is America. It is not like San Francisco. . . . But at first it did frighten me too. I felt like an ant. But I like some American ways.

The women, for instance, wearing expensive fur coats and . . . boots on their feet and scarfs on their heads! No Italian woman would do that, no matter how cold it was—she would be afraid she would not look chic. I like the American way. It's practical."

An Italian restaurant on West 54th Street was recommended to the two Tebaldis—even the name of it was familiar to them: it is called La Scala. Except for lunches and dinners there and trips to the Metropolitan for Renata's rehearsals they did not go anywhere; they just remained quietly in their apartment at the hotel.

But Renata could not keep her mind on anything else —we had to talk about the Met. She told me how shocked she was when she saw its exterior. She could not believe her eyes. She was used to the beautiful buildings of La Scala and the other opera houses in Italy, of the Paris Opera, of the photographs of the Vienna Opera House. By comparison the Met did not look any better than an old cinema. She felt better once she entered the building —it did look familiar, although larger than most others. Still, she thought, the auditorium was much too old, much too heavy—*pesante*—and the colors of the walls and the seats are somber, depressing. She was told by her colleagues that certain sections in the house have poor acoustics, but her worst surprise came when she was shown the dressing rooms. She had never seen anything so shabby in any opera house before. "And this in the wealthiest city in the world!"

"But," and she raised her forefinger, "it must be a wonderful opera house. So far as I can judge from the few rehearsals." Renata was impressed by the strict discipline and the serious attitude of everyone concerned with the production.

"And one had better be on time for rehearsals—five minutes before eleven in the morning. They have none of this strolling in half an hour later. No star system, no special privileges." Renata always liked efficiency and a serious attitude toward work, and if strict discipline is necessary to achieve this, then she is all for it.

Although Renata was the first important Italian soprano in fifteen years to make her debut at the Met, she was not heralded by any special fanfare. Quite the contrary, only here and there in the musical magazines were there a few lines mentioning her forthcoming appearance, the most extravagant of them saying: "Her voice which has so far been out of the Metropolitan Opera is close to being out of this world also, according to reports."

But the Monday night of January 31, 1955, turned into a gala—the largest crowd the auditorium could hold consisted of musicians, music lovers, and society people who were curious to see "the most beautiful woman on the stage," as more than one critic has called her. According to the management the demand for tickets was even greater than for Marian Anderson's debut there shortly before. Every singer and every music critic in town was

154

there, and the passionate discussions during the intermission reminded one of the stock exchange at its busiest
hour.

The audience was prepared to welcome Renata and
they did so in royal fashion, giving her an ovation at the
end of the performance. It was unfortunate, however,
that Renata's first night at the Met was perhaps not
under the best circumstances. *Otello* had not been given
for two years, and although Mr. Bing had selected the
best forces to accompany Renata's Desdemona—Mario
del Monaco as Otello, Leonard Warren as Iago, and had
entrusted the leading of the opera to Fritz Stiedry, an
experienced conductor, and the staging to Dino Yannopoulos—the production was far from satisfying. The
orchestra was much too loud, Stiedry's cues and tempi
often uncertain and uneven. Apparently directed by
Yannopoulos, who was trying to be too realistic, the
tenor overplayed his role at times. Gesticulating violently
and throwing too many people down on the stage too
many times, his behavior resembled more that of a common ruffian than of the essentially noble Otello. (In later
performances he improved greatly and is today an out-
standing Otello.)

But the audience came not so much to hear the opera
Otello, as it did to hear Renata Tebaldi. It would be naive
to think that it lacked sound critical judgment. But New
Yorkers are not easily prompted to boo, on the contrary
they prefer to overlook small mishaps and hope for the

best. This was obvious in their attitude toward Renata, who was very nervous. They understood well what caused it—the importance of her New York debut, the often erratic conducting of Stiedry, the unfamiliar orchestra, stage, and the audience.

As she began to sing Renata sounded a little uncertain but she soon got hold of herself and as the performance progressed she gained more and more assurance until she revealed the full beauty of her voice, its range and power, poised, unstrained, with chiseled distinction. In the last act she sang the "Salce, salce," and the "Ave Maria" with so much richness and warmth that it was worthy of the highest praise of the most severe critics. These two numbers alone showed why she has often been compared with such legendary sopranos as Galli-Curci and Claudia Muzio. The ovation she received was so tumultuous that some cynics suspected a claque, but the management insisted that these stout-handed opera fans were applauding for love, not money.

Renata was delighted with her enthusiastic reception by the audience and the press. But she was puzzled by the fact that some critics left the Met before the last act of *Otello* in order to meet a deadline. This was incomprehensible to her. "Do they never stay to the end of the opera? How can they tell what has happened?"

But above all she was pleased with a handwritten letter from Toscanini, who was in Italy, wishing her triumphant success.

Renata was sincerely surprised by the many flowers she received. She did not know she had so many admirers in New York. But she was even more mystified by a strange man who had sent her a box of red roses and a bottle of champagne. Before going on stage Renata drank a little of the champagne—for good luck. After the performance a tall elderly man dressed in a white tie, top hat, and an opera cape came backstage to congratulate her. He behaved in the most dignified manner, kissed her hand, said a few pleasant words, and departed. Later, Renata told me, she heard that he was one of the regular operagoers, who never missed a night if he could help it. And indeed he came to congratulate Renata after every performance. She became so used to it that when he failed to come after one of the performances and then again after the second, Renata tried to learn what was amiss. She was told that he must have died. Renata never managed to find out just who the mysterious man was.

During the next six weeks Renata sang *Otello* four times more, and *La Bohème, Andrea Chenier,* and *Tosca* one performance each. This gave ample opportunity to those critics who did not make up their minds on the first hearing to warm up to Renata. They learned more about her as an artist while she became better acquainted with her audiences and seemed to have won them with her simple and sincere way. Even her lack of knowledge of English often served as an asset. She was to sing her first *Tosca* for the benefit of the Milk Fund for children. Renata quite earnestly explained to a reporter that *Tosca* was a very Italian opera and very emotional, but that she was sure that the babies would like it. When she was told that the "babies" seldom attended this performance, Renata was visibly chagrined—but the reporters were charmed.

Happy with her new conquest, Renata returned in the spring of 1955 to Italy to fulfill her engagements there, among them La Scala in Milan. There, having made her decision to leave the opera house, she sang her last *Forza del Destino*, hoping that her road and that of Madame Callas would never again cross. But this was not to be. She returned in August to the United States for a concert at the Hollywood Bowl and several performances at the San Francisco Opera. And in October she came to Chicago to make her debut there in *Aida*.

For two weeks starting on October 31, as *Time* magazine said, the Chicago Lyric Theatre managed to present Renata Tebaldi and Maria Callas on alternate nights.

The season opened with Callas singing Elvira in Bellini's old-fashioned *I Puritani,* its creakiness made tolerable only by her vocal pyrotechnics and the affecting understatement of her dramatic approach. The next night Tebaldi sang the title role of Verdi's *Aida,* and critics and audience surrendered to her big voice and finely spun pianissimo. Mme Callas subsequently tackled Verdi's *Il Trovatore* and Mme Tebaldi took on Puccini's *La Bohème.*

There were no hisses, no hair-pulling after this combat and Renata returned to New York in one piece, safe and sound, ready to start her season at the Met, including the Metropolitan Opera tour, which revealed her to audiences in Cleveland, Richmond, Atlanta, Memphis, Dallas, Houston, Minneapolis, Bloomington, Chicago, Toronto, and Montreal, in the spring of the following year.

-- *Chapter 13* --

"And what now?" she asked wistfully when I saw her before she went back to Italy. "I have sung everywhere in Italy, and I have sung in Paris, London, Rio de Janeiro, Edinburgh, Lisbon, Los Angeles, San Francisco and New York. I would like to sing in Vienna, but then what? What should I do afterwards?" She sounded as if she had passed the summit of her career, but far from being the end of her public life it was only the beginning. And indeed now she has had to add to her heavy schedule of appearances in Europe her yearly visits to this country.

It would be monotonous to report in detail the evidence of her constantly growing popularity on both continents. Instead of following her from one opera house to another during the next two years, I have decided to bring together in this chapter conversations I have had with her about the way she conceives and studies her roles and some of her critical reflections about certain operas. From her extensive repertoire, I have selected only those opera roles which most characteristically illustrate her particular methods.

Renata has told me that the basis for her knowledge of dramatic action was laid by Carmen Melis while she was still her pupil at the Conservatory in Pesaro. Melis had an extraordinary gift of characterization, but what was even more important, she had the ability to transmit her ideas to her students. Renata came to her knowing nothing about the stage, nothing about acting, and was so fascinated by Melis that she would be the first to arrive at her class each day and would sit in the first row without ever taking her eyes off Melis, without missing a single word. She says that she still remembers every gesture, every movement, every step Melis took.

During one of her first lessons Melis had shown her pupils how to portray the difference in Marguerite's mood in two scenes in Gounod's *Faust:* one, while sitting at the spinning wheel, and the other when she plays with the jewels in front of the mirror.

Later on, of course, as Renata developed her own

161

technique of expression, she often did not use exactly the same gestures—those more natural to Melis than to herself—but she always tried to preserve the basic conception which she learned from Melis.

There is nothing new in saying that the utmost concentration is imperative while composing a role, and Renata says that for days she thinks of nothing else, until the character becomes completely her own. That is, until she can practically identify herself with the person she is playing. Renata did and still does all the composing of her mind, before rehearsals. Speaking in general of her method of studying, she said that she works out in her mind not only the over-all conception of the part, but also every detail of the action: "I am much too timid to do it in my room, or, as I understand a great many singers and actors do, in front of a mirror. I would be much too self-conscious to practice gestures and movements even if I were alone in the room, and certainly I could never do it with anyone present—not even Mamma. So you see it is a problem, which I have to solve by imagining everything I put later into action. But once I have memorized the sequence of action, so to speak, then I am ready for a rehearsal with a stage director, and I follow him as long as his interpretation corresponds more or less with my own. But whether I agree with a particular stage director's interpretations or not I certainly have learned a great deal from them."

Renata worked with Gioacchino Forzano in Rome, and

with Aldo Mirabella Vassallo on *La Traviata* as well as on *Andrea Chenier, Madama Butterfly,* and *Manon Lescaut.* These operas she did with him in Palermo, Naples, and Catania. She worked with Tatyana Pavlova on *Eugene Onegin* for La Scala, and with Herbert Graf on Handel's *Giulio Cesare* at the Roman amphitheater in Pompeii. Later with Pierre Bertin from the Comédie Française she restudied *Andrea Chenier.* Renata also worked with Roberto Rossellini in Naples on *Otello,* but she does not think much of him. "He may be a good motion picture director," she says, "but he knows nothing about music and is not good at directing an opera."

Renata believes that there is no use in trying to act any role until you know every note of your singing part, every nuance in the musical interpretation so well that you do not need to think about it. This is the most important prerequisite.

She also believes that acting should be realistic—the audience must be made to feel that the actor or the singer is indeed the character he is personifying. She admits, however, that if in some parts which she sings, she sometimes cries with real tears, it is because the particular episode somehow by association of ideas brings to her mind something that has happened in her own life. And some roles she feels so intently that the performance leaves her completely exhausted, *morta.*

We spoke about two different schools of acting. As an example, I told her a story that Feodor Chaliapin's son

163

Boris, a talented painter, told me. Once while his father was acting in a most pathetic scene in *Don Quichotte,* which Massenet wrote for him, he suddenly noticed his son watching him from the wings. At that particular moment the singer was on his knees crying, but he not only managed to wink at his son with the eye which was not visible to the public, but to actually whisper his name *"Borka, Borka . . ."* without interrupting his histrionics.

Also, according to Harold Schoenberg, the *New York Times* music critic, during a performance of *Aida,* after George London had finished a solo passage, Zinka Milanov turned her back to the audience and whispered: "George, how is the new baby? I understand she's a darling."

Renata realized that they believed in "acting" the roles, not "living" them. She said that this approach would be much easier—"one would not need to use up so much of one's self."

Since several characters in the operas which she sings are supposed to die in the last act, Renata has made quite a study of a person's behavior at his death. It may sound naive, but she is convinced that a woman who dies of poison, for instance, dies in quite a different way from one who dies of an illness or of a broken heart. To illustrate her point she spoke of the varying deaths of Violetta in *La Traviata,* Mimi in *La Bohème,* Cio-Cio San in *Madama Butterfly* and Adriana Lecouvreur in Cilea's opera. Renata consulted doctors about these matters. She said that in some cases a dying person is "something like the light of a candle which slowly goes out."

Renata worked for a long time on *La Traviata* before she felt she could do justice to the role of Violetta. At first she read carefully Alexandre Dumas' *La Dame aux Camélias*. Then, in 1950 she went specially to Venice to see Edwige Feuillère, a famous French actress who played the title role in the play. "But," Renata said, "great as her performance was, it only convinced me of what I had been thinking all along: it would be a great mistake to try to act the role of Violetta in the opera as one would do it in the play. In opera everything is governed and also limited by the music. You cannot take liberties with the time, you cannot, for instance, have long pauses for the sake of a dramatic effect, as you can in a play. This is also true of *Tosca,* and I believe it would be true of any opera which was first conceived as a dramatic play."

In order to feel confident in her portrayal of the death scene she discussed the whole process of tuberculosis with her fiancé Antonio, then a student of medicine.

"During the last stage of the illness," Renata said, "tubercular people are practically unconscious of what they are doing or saying, and finally go out like the light of a candle." This last description seems to picture to her particularly well the quiet, slow death of Violetta, for Renata often quoted this same phrase.

She told me that she likes *La Traviata* for its "human" element. "It could have happened anywhere, at any time, it could have happened yesterday or today, and it certainly will happen over and over again."

She has always been fascinated by the complete change in Violetta's character as we see her in the different acts of the opera, and of course she was impressed by the tremendous, as she called it, sacrifice made by Violetta. "I also love the opera because of the music's descriptiveness. Every prelude and entr'acte puts the audience in the mood of the following action and prepares it for what is going to happen."

Since the conception of Violetta's personality has long become traditional, Renata does not think that her own interpretation is very different from those of others, except, and here she likes to emphasize her point, she does not believe that Violetta was at any time merely a vulgar courtesan, as some singers sometimes portray her.

Actually Renata has not had the opportunity to see many different Violettas. She had heard about Rosina Storchio, the famous Italian soprano, who was known for her remarkable performance of this role. A great beauty, Storchio sang at La Scala at the end of the last century and the beginning of this one. Of course Renata never saw her. But she has heard some records made by another famous Violetta—Gemma Bellincioni. From what she learned about Storchio, Renata is inclined to believe that Bellincioni was even better in the role. She died in 1950 in Naples.

As I have mentioned several times, Renata is always

166

nervous on the day of her performance, but when she used to sing in *La Traviata,* she felt worse than ever. Then, she would prolong her morning in bed, take a long time over her breakfast, and dawdle getting dressed. Next, she would go to church. (Whenever she arrives in a strange town, the first thing she does is to find a Catholic church. She does not like to pray in large cathedrals. She prefers the small, intimate churches, which have far more atmosphere, she says.) At the church she would leave three candles: one for the Sacred Heart, one for St. Anthony of Padua, and one for the Madonna.

On her *La Traviata* night she would go to the theater early, even earlier than usual, to see that everything was in order, her costumes, her hairdresser ready for her. Then she would start to make up, but again she would do it very slowly and carefully. On her dressing table, besides her mother's picture, she keeps three holy pictures. Before she goes on stage she kneels before them and prays once more. "Only then do I lose my nervousness," she confided to me, but after a pause she added: "No, frankly, I don't lose it entirely until I am on the stage and begin to sing."

During her 1956 season at the Met, besides her appearances in *La Bohème* and *Tosca,* she sang in *La Traviata.* Her debut in this opera on February 21 in a new production especially created for her had such a success that she gave eight more performances of it at the Met, one in Boston, and one in Baltimore, and when in the spring of the same year she went with the Metropolitan Opera Company on a tour of some twelve cities, she sang the part ten more times.

If she ever had to prove to herself or "others" her ability in the role of Violetta, these performances should have sufficed.

"And now I shall never sing *La Traviata* again," Renata told me. She looked sad. "My voice has grown too big for the part."

After one of her performances of *Tosca* we had a long discussion about the opera.

"I loved *Tosca* from the first time I heard it," Renata told me, "but you know, I don't think that Floria Tosca's personality grips the audience until the second act. Although in the first act all the other roles are well drawn— Scarpia and Cavaradossi, and even Tosca seems to be well presented—somehow I feel she does not have a chance to show her character completely."

Renata has never seen Victorien Sardou's play from which the opera was derived, and had never heard of Sarah Bernhardt's creation of the famous role. Originally Renata studied the dramatic action of the role with Carmen Melis, herself a famous Tosca, but both Melis and Renata told me that her present interpretation has evolved from her experience with many stage directors. Her latest *Tosca* was directed by Margarita Wallmann, the present stage director at La Scala. Wallmann introduced some new stage business—mere details in themselves, but Renata has adopted them. In the second act in Scarpia's palazzo she comes in wearing a thin stole made of the same material as her dress. When she stabs Scarpia, he catches the stole and pulls it to himself. But although she manages to extricate herself, no matter how much she tries to release the scarf from Scarpia it remains in his firm grip and when she finally gives up the struggle his fist, clutching it, as he dies, falls back on the floor with a resounding thud.

"Also, a few minutes later," Renata added, "instead of blowing out the candles, I put out the light by lightly tapping the wicks with the ends of my fingers—one, two, three, four, five."

Of all her roles Renata believes that Desdemona's part in *Otello* suits her best—vocally as well as dramatically. She says that it suits her own temperament, timid and romantic, and yet it is the only role which does not completely satisfy her, because she cannot identify with Desdemona in her submission to Otello's jealousy. (This from Renata, one of the most jealous of women!) She told me that sometimes it makes her laugh and she has a hard time controlling herself on the stage.

Vocally Desdemona's part is one of the best for her, and for this reason among others Melis advised her always to make her debut in new cities in *Otello*. When she sang her first Desdemona in Trieste in December, 1946, Merli, famous for his Otello, sang with her. She worked with him on the dramatic action at Madame Scalvini's apartment in Milan.

But Renata's greatest experience in dramatic action was her study of the role of Madama Butterfly with the Japanese stage director, Yoshio Aoyama, shortly before her first performance of *Madama Butterfly* at the Met on November 8, 1958.

Aoyama at one time was a dancer in the famous Japanese Kabuki ballet. When Renata met him in New York he was in his early fifties. "He is tall for a Japanese, about five foot six," Renata said as she described him. "He has graying hair, wears glasses, which give him a stern appearance. He is slender, and well but simply dressed. He spoke practically no English and therefore we had to work with two interpreters—his own who translated from the Japanese into English, and mine, who translated further for me into Italian. But soon after we began working together, I felt that there was no barrier because of the language. Often I would instinctively understand what he said before it was translated to me."

When they met, Aoyama greeted her in the European way, kissing her hand. Renata said that he smiled only occasionally and usually spoke to her in a businesslike way.

As soon as they started to work Aoyama, his interpreter, and Renata would put on kimonos. Renata also had to learn to wear the flat Japanese sandals which have a special arrangement for the big toes. Japanese women wear stockings especially cut that way. At the beginning Renata found the wearing of them very painful, and to get used to them she had to practice wearing them in her apartment in New York. Several times a day she would put them on and try to learn to walk in them.

After the first lesson she was so discouraged that she cried—she was convinced that she could never learn to do what Aoyama asked for. "It was so different from anything I knew about the role." But Renata was determined and during the following ten days she worked with him for two hours every day, sometimes twice a day.

"To show you how far back I had to go—I literally had to learn how to walk," Renata smiled. "The Japanese women don't walk in the way we do. They don't put their feet on the ground in the same way. Since from their childhood they are used to wearing flat sandals their feet actually are turned outward. This turns the body slightly to one side, almost in a crooked way. But as they also tilt their heads to the same side, it gives them a very feminine and coquettish appearance.

"Then Mr. Aoyama explained to me how my face should be made up in order to resemble a Japanese woman. The Japanese woman's face is very white. She has almost no eyebrows, just two thin short lines. These are close to her nose; there are no hairs near the temple. Her mouth is small and is in the shape of a heart. The lids of the eyes are low and heavy and she has almost no

171

eyelashes. As a rule the Japanese women have no hair on their bodies.

"After that Mr. Aoyama taught me how to wear a kimono, how to walk into a room and how to sit down on the floor in such a way that the kimono would not open in front. There are two different kinds of kimonos: those for everyday wear, and those for ceremonial occasions. The everyday kimonos have shorter sleeves. The others, intended for festive occasions, are much larger and more luxurious. Japanese women never wear any kind of ornament. A flower in their hair is all that they allow themselves. They never wear any kind of jewelry, neither on their arms and hands, nor around their necks—no rings, no bracelets, no necklaces. In fact they are not supposed to show their hands or their wrists to a man, a stranger. With their fingers they pick up the end of the kimono sleeve in such a way that it hardly shows their hands. Then they hold their arms pulled upward toward their heads so that they look almost crippled. But, as I have said, with their heads slightly turned to one side, this produces a rather feminine effect.

"Their behavior, attitudes, movements and gestures are entirely different from ours. The use of the fan is very important. Japanese fans are different—they are much harder to handle than others. But they permit a very characteristic gesture: the closing of the fan with a short staccato clicking sound. From the way she uses her fan one can almost distinguish to which social class a woman belongs. Geishas, for instance, use their wrists with a more undulating, more coquettish movement than women from an aristocratic family, whose emotions and gestures are far more restrained. Another characteristic gesture is to cover a part of the face, up to the eyes, with an open fan."

It somehow resembled the effect of a Turkish *chadra* or veil, I suggested, and Renata agreed.

Renata told me that the technique of using the fan sometimes reaches a real virtuosity, such as, for instance, when dancers throw an open fan up into the air, catch it, and begin to use it.

"All our European gestures accompanying our speech are completely foreign to the Japanese," Renata went on. "For instance, when they count, they don't point at each finger, but close each one toward the palm of the hand after it is counted. When Madama Butterfly says, 'He promised to return,' she accompanies the word 'promised' by crossing the index fingers of her two hands—one above the other.

"Finally," Renata said, "while working with Mr. Aoyama I discovered that certain things had to be changed in Puccini's directions, as well as in his score. When Cio-Cio San calls her maid, who happens to be in the same room, she should not clap her hands. It is different, however, if they happen to be in a garden.

"The death scene as described by Puccini is wrong and really should be altered. No Japanese woman would commit hara-kiri. Only men do. She commits suicide in a different way. She places herself on her haunches, ties her kimono tight around her waist, and ties her dress above her knees with a piece of cloth, as if it were a belt. This has to be done carefully, for it must be so tight that her body cannot move. Then she places a dagger with its blade turned upward on the ground before her and throws herself in such way that the blade will strike her heart.

"No Japanese woman would kill herself with her child in the room, as Puccini directs in his score. As you know, according to Puccini, the child is supposed to be blind-folded by Madama Butterfly and left sitting while she kills herself. No Japanese woman would commit suicide in the presence of anybody, and certainly not in front of her child. She would have to be alone. Thus, I believe that this part in Puccini's stage directions should be altered." Of course these directions were taken by the librettists from the original play by David Belasco.

On the whole, Renata thinks that Puccini's music does not suit a Japanese woman, who would be much too restrained to show any emotion and would hardly sing such passionate arias.

I said that everything is possible in opera, but Renata did not agree: "*Madama Butterfly* is much too realistic a story and therefore should be kept in that framework. I have heard the famous Japanese Madama Butterfly,

Hizi Koyke," Renata said. "She came to Rome. She could sing the notes and most probably she interpreted the role according to the Japanese nature and understood Puccini's music, but it was not the Italian Puccini. It was not Italian music. But I hear that the Japanese like Italian music, and curiously enough they seem even to like *Madama Butterfly* despite the story toward which they obviously cannot have full sympathy. I have heard that they give the opera quite often."

Originally Renata studied *Madama Butterfly* with Carmen Melis, but because of her size, she never felt secure in this role—she thought she was much too tall for it.

"I feel differently now. It may sound funny, but Mr. Aoyama's teaching reduced my size, if I may say so. He taught me how to produce the effect of a small and dainty little woman."

After ten days of working with him, Aoyama declared that Renata was ready for the role. But it still costs her tears, and she is *morta* after each performance of *Madama Butterfly*.

Renata told me that she does not have "favorite" roles, that she likes different parts for different reasons, some of them perhaps because they are better suited for her voice and temperament, but this does not entirely determine her feelings for them. Naturally she prefers the Italian operas—she sings only in Italian. She says that French is too nasal, and German too guttural for her. In

175

general I believe that after Italian music she likes best the Russian. (She has sung Tatyana in Tchaikovsky's *Eugene Onegin* at La Scala.)

I have noticed that she prefers romantic music, but favors Chopin, Tchaikovsky and Rachmaninoff more than Schumann. Certainly she is not particularly interested in the modern composers. If a composition lacks *bel canto* passages it seems to cease to be music for her. But so far she has not given contemporary music a fair chance. She has not heard enough to get used to the new idiom.

Renata does not go to as many concerts as she should and would like to. This she regrets and excuses herself by lack of time. During the concert season she is too busy herself. She is also sorry that she no longer plays the piano. She could not bear playing badly and to play well you have to practice, she says, and for that she has no patience.

— Chapter 14 —

On Renata's trip to the United States in 1957 she and her mother were accompanied by Ernestina Vigano, a twenty-five-year-old Italian girl. Tina, as she is affectionately called by everybody, has been an admirer of Renata since she was seventeen years old, when from her seat in the gallery at La Scala she heard Renata in *Otello*. Like most of Renata's young fans she wrote and asked for Renata's photograph—this was the beginning of a relationship which eventually developed into the most sincere and devoted friendship between Tina and the two Tebaldis.

Tina is the youngest member of a large family who live in Monza, where she was born and where she used to work in a bakery shop. But Tina loves music and learned to play the piano a little. When she began to follow Renata's performances, she became infatuated with the singer's voice and was willing to do anything, to serve in any capacity as long as she could be near Renata and hear her sing. This, in fact, she told Giuseppina, and from about 1951 on, Giuseppina often called on her to come to Milan to help her with many chores, mostly connected with taking care of Renata's costumes and clothes. To be Renata's *costumista* was just what Tina dreamed of, and in this capacity she became the constant companion of the Tebaldis.

During that fall while Renata was singing at the Chicago Opera, she caught the grippe. She is convinced that she had the Asiatic flu. At that time it was fashionable to call every cold the Asiatic flu. At any rate, before long all of them, that is Renata, Giuseppina, Renata's secretary, and Tina were put to bed. But the Asiatic flu did not seem to last very long or to leave any perceptible effect, and they returned to New York where Renata was scheduled to start her annual performances at the Met. They arrived at their Buckingham Hotel apartment on November 17, the day before Giuseppina's birthday.

They spent the festive day quietly at home. Giuseppina received many presents and flowers from their friends, and in the evening as usual they dined *en famille* at La

178

Scala restaurant. Next day Giuseppina complained of nausea. Renata attributed this to indigestion, but when later on her mother told her of a pain in her chest and back, Renata called in a doctor. The young doctor who examined Giuseppina said that there was nothing to worry about, he saw nothing seriously wrong with her, but he said that perhaps it would be advisable for her to come to his office to have an electrocardiogram made.

On the following day Giuseppina felt worse. She did not want to go out to see the same young doctor. Instead Renata telephoned to Dr. Claudio Gerbi, an Italian physician who had always attended Renata in New York. He recognized at once the seriousness of Giuseppina's condition. Later he returned with the E.C.G. apparatus. He diagnosed an attack of coronary thrombosis. Although Renata's mother had become semi-conscious and remained so during the following three days, the doctor told Renata that it might not be fatal. Often, he said, a patient recovers and lives a long time afterwards.

Giuseppina had a strong constitution. Otherwise perfectly healthy, she had been suffering from diabetes, but she took good care of herself—kept a strict diet, and regularly took insulin. However, as Renata's constant companion Giuseppina also led a very strenuous life: she took charge of everything connected with her daughter's nomadic existence. Just to see to it that all the paraphernalia of a traveling prima donna got to its destination on time involved everlasting packing, unpacking and repacking, and the living in hotels between trains or boats and cooking whenever it was possible, with special meals for herself and Renata, would have tired any one. But even aside from all these purely functional occupations Giuseppina's nervous system was constantly strained. Sitting in the wings of the various opera houses, she lived through every note Renata ever sang in public, and every performance no doubt cost her as much health as it did Renata. Thus her own suffering from diabetes, aggravated by her nervous condition, may have contributed to the weakening of her heart. And indeed, just before they left Italy for this last trip, Giuseppina was told by her doctor in Milan that her heart was not as good as it should be. But of course none of them expected that her condition could so soon and so suddenly become so grave.

At first Tina tried to shield Renata from the truth of the situation, but it was only a matter of hours before Renata realized what was happening. She canceled her *Tosca* performance which was to take place on November 21. Mr. Bing came to plead with her, but Renata shook her head. She would fulfill her commitment only on one condition: someone would have to keep in touch with her mother's sick room, and if Giuseppina's condition became worse, she would have to be informed at once even if she were on the stage, and she would leave immediately to be at her mother's side. She knew that this was an unacceptable condition, but this was one

instance when the strictly disciplined singer Renata Tebaldi was subservient to Rena, Giuseppina's only child.

Two days later Giuseppina had a second attack. Dr.
Gerbi suggested calling a priest. He also advised taking
Giuseppina to a hospital, but Renata would not hear of
that. Renata had engaged two nurses, but as harrowing
as it was for her to watch her mother die, she would not
think of leaving her bedside. Besides, whenever Giuseppina would regain consciousness for a short while, she
always called for Renata or Tina, and Renata would
never have forgiven herself if both had not been there,
even if it meant to be tormented by hearing her mother
repeating over and over again: "*Addio . . . Addio . . .*"

The agony started on November 29, and by five the
next morning Giuseppina Tebaldi was gone.

Her mother's death was the greatest tragedy in Renata's life. She was literally stunned by it. All her life her
heart had beat in unison with her mother's. But deep as
was her grief, Renata kept it under control. When Linda
Barone, an Italian girl, at one time her secretary, walked
into Renata's room several hours later, Renata was in bed.
"Pina died," was all she said.

In the afternoon Cardinal Spellman came to see her
and had a long talk with her. He had known the Tebaldis
for some time. While Giuseppina was ill he had called on
her several times and now he came to share Renata's loss.
Renata spoke quietly—she doubted if she would ever

181

sing again. But Cardinal Spellman dissuaded her from such thoughts. As a true Christian, he told her, she owed to God to fulfill her duty and use her talents on the appointed path.

But Renata felt forlorn, utterly alone. There was no one whom she considered close friends except Tina, and Signor Luigi Rovescala, an elderly man, an old friend of the family, who came from Milan as soon as he heard about Giuseppina's condition, and Linda Barone. Alone of them, Miss Barone spoke English and could be of help to Renata. A former graduate student of literature at the university in her native town of Florence, twice in previous years she had joined Renata as her secretary on trips to London and the United States. She was used to handling Renata's correspondence and some of her business affairs. But it was Cardinal Spellman's personal assistance that expedited everything involved with the transportation of Giuseppina's remains for burial in Langhirano.

Renata was always terrified of flying, but now she asked to have the coffin sent at once to Italy by air. She would fly on the same plane, she said. This plan, however, had to be abandoned after two days of fruitless effort—according to Italian Government regulations, the original zinc coffin had to be encased in a second, wooden coffin, to prevent any damage. Since it was too large to go into the baggage compartment of the Alitalia plane on which Renata wanted to go home, Signor Soreno, the president of the company, hoped that it could be placed in the regular passenger compartment. But even by unhinging the door of the plane it would not go through. Therefore the coffin eventually was turned over to a TWA cargo plane, while Renata, accompanied by Signor Rovescala and Tina, were to follow it on the Italian plane.

Although a snowstorm delayed Renata's departure for a day, she saw the coffin at the airport in Shannon where it was being transferred to another cargo plane. For two days after Renata's arrival in Milan no one knew, nor could anyone find out, what had happened to the coffin. Finally during the night of December 5 Renata was informed that the plane had just landed in Turin, one hundred and thirty-two kilometers, some eighty miles, southwest of Milan, and that she would have to send a hearse to transport the coffin to Milan. She was also told that someone would have to come to identify Giuseppina's body before it could leave the airport.

On the following day, after Giuseppina's remains were at last brought to the former apartment of the Tebaldis in Langhirano where friends could come to pay their last respects, a short service was held at the little church where Renata as a child used to sing in the choir. Then, followed practically by the whole of Langhirano and by many who came from Milan, the procession walked slowly to the small cemetery of Mattaleto.

After the funeral Renata spent the night at her cousin

Tilde's and next day returned to her apartment in Milan. It was then that the harrowing experience of the past two weeks broke down Renata's resistance.

There were rumors in the United States that in her despair Renata had vowed to give up singing and enter a convent. This was not true. On the contrary Cardinal Spellman's words reminded her once more that only her public life could assuage her pain—this as a true artist she knew, and after two months of quiet at home she went to Barcelona to keep an engagement there: three performances of *Madama Butterfly,* and one of *La Bohème*.

"You once remarked," Renata said to me two years later as we sat looking through some old and new snapshots, "that I changed from a girl into a woman in 1956. No, I think that it was with Mamma's death that I ceased to be a young girl. I suddenly realized how much she meant to me and how dependent I had been on her. And now I was alone in the big world in which I was living."

But Renata was not entirely alone. There was Tina. "Soon after the funeral," Tina told me, "the Signorina asked me if I would stay with her. I never thought of leaving her. Her mother told me many times during her life, and also when she was dying, never to leave the Signorina. And I am not going to."

Tina's devotion to Renata is as unselfish and strong as that which bound Renata and her mother. She knows no other life but the one of taking care of Renata. And today she is more than just her *costumista*. She is Renata's confidante, and Renata trusts her advice, for Tina has a re-markable intuitive judgment of people and situations.

Speaking of this new friendship of Renata's, Carmen Melis said to me: "If anyone wants to remain friends with Renata, he had better be good to Tina."

-- *Chapter 15* --

Despite the fact that after Giuseppina's death Renata canceled all six performances she was scheduled for at the Met from November 21 to December 24, 1957, which was very disappointing for the management, Rudolf Bing, most probably to show his admiration for her, reserved the opening night of the following season for Renata in *Tosca*. It was a gala performance, as all first nights at the Met are, and it also had an aura of solemnity, as if the audience were paying once more a tribute to Renata's love and devotion to her mother.

Even more important was December 9, 1959, in Renata's career and personal life. On that night she returned to La Scala after an absence of four and a half years. She had left La Scala in the spring of 1955 after her last performance of *La Forza del Destino*. As she said then, it was a hard decision for her to make but she had no choice —she was not going to sing in any theater, no matter how dear to her, where Madame Callas reigned.

But Madame Callas's reign did not last long. Two years later, in September 1957, during a visit to Edinburgh as a member of the Scala company which was invited to participate in the festival there, Madame Callas refused to remain for an extra performance of Bellini's *La Sonnambula*, and went instead to a party given by Elsa Maxwell in Venice. Apparently the fact that Madame Callas had fulfilled the number of performances stipulated in her contract did not justify her conduct in the eyes of the management of La Scala. They felt she should have been willing because of her success at the festival to fulfill the request for one extra performance. Then in January of the following year in Rome her *Norma* was booed and she left the theater after the first act. This aroused the indignation of the Italian people, particularly because the President of the Republic was attending the performance. It was taken as an insult to him. The Rome incident put a final touch to the feelings at La Scala, and Madame Callas seems to have come out of these two escapades with the scepter dropped from her hand and her crown slightly askew.

While Renata was in no hurry to go back to La Scala, the Milanese were anxious to have her and used the first opportunity to show it. After Renata's concert for UNI-CEF at the Manzoni Theater in 1956 they carried the ovation into the street where, surrounding Renata's car, they pushed it along the Via Manzoni all the way to La Scala shouting: "Renata, we want to hear you at La Scala." And after they reached the opera house they continued their demonstration, chanting how impatient they were to hear her there, and showering more flowers into a car already filled with blossoms.

Since the first opening in her busy schedule was at the beginning of the season 1959–1960, Renata agreed to this date to appear at La Scala. But, although she was offered the first night, she preferred to appear three days later. "Of course it would have been a great honor for me to open the season at La Scala, and I appreciated the offer, but I would have had to sing in *Otello,* and it is actually a tenor's opera. That is why I chose to forego the honor of the first night and to sing *Tosca,* where the soprano has the title role."

As the date of Renata's forthcoming return to La Scala approached the old partisans, the Tebaldiani and the Callasiani, were preparing to start the old controversy. Madame Callas, however, supplied them with the wrong ammunition: during the previous summer months she made headlines in newspapers all over the world, but unfortunately for the Callasiani, not by her appearances on the stage of an opera house but on Mr. Onassis' yacht in the Mediterranean. It was purely Madame Callas' personal affair and could not possibly be of any importance to anyone except those who were directly concerned. Soon afterwards Madame Callas came to Milan on account of her matrimonial troubles, and she used the opportunity to see Mr. Ghiringhelli to try to patch up the "misunderstandings" which were created by the Edinburgh and Rome incidents. The results of these discussions, however, did not make the headlines.

Nor did Renata supply her admirers with any startling news. As I have related before, she spent the month of July and the first part of August 1959 in Rome recording. Then during the month of September she went to Vienna where she was to appear in several operas and to record *Aida*, but because she was overworked and needed a rest she returned to Milan, still hoping to fulfill her commitments for a tour in Germany.

Musicians in Milan seemed to have been more concerned about Renata's return to La Scala than she herself was. "What is the matter with her?" they would ask me. "Doesn't she realize how important her appearance at La Scala is for her career? How can she insist on going on a tour in Germany?" Renata was the only one who was extremely calm about it. I saw her constantly during the summer months but she never mentioned her date at La Scala to me. And I am convinced that when on the advice of her doctors she finally canceled her German tour, she did so not because of her future appearance at La Scala, but because she did not want to go to Germany when she was not in her best voice. She remained quietly in her apartment in Milan and in November went to Barcelona for more performances. Before returning to Milan she was to sing in *Andrea Chenier* at the San Carlo in Naples, but she caught the grippe and had to cancel her appearances in *Andriana Lecouvreur*.

Thus all the Tebaldiani and Callasiani could do was watch the rainy skies so bad for singers. And they said in Milan that while Renata was rehearsing *Tosca,* Madame Callas was seen on the narrow streets and in the small restaurants near La Scala looking like Medea.

It would be naive to think that Renata was not aware of the situation—"It was very strenuous for my nerves. After all I know how many people are against me." (She meant the Callasiani.) But she did not need to worry.

La Scala was packed and one could easily distinguish in the hall the warring partisans by their nervous gestures and loud cries, but in all fairness to the Callasiani one must say that they made no attempt to disturb the apparent festive atmosphere. In tense excitement the audience watched the beginning of the opera. But when Mario Cavaradossi, having promised to help Cesare Angelotti, the fugitive political plotter, returned to his painting, and Tosca's voice was heard calling from backstage "Mario! Mario! Mario!" the three thousand people who had held their breaths until then suddenly lost control.

"*Ecco, è lei!*" was heard like a distant sound of thunder through the house. "There she is!" And when a few seconds later Renata Tebaldi appeared on the stage, all in the audience jumped to their feet, applauding and shouting her name, welcoming her back to La Scala and wishing her to remain there forever. It was a great surge of admiration and love. The tumultuous ovation lasted so long that Tosca's first dialogue with Cavaradossi was completely blotted out by the delirious cries of the public—extraordinary behavior in a theater where applause during the acts is strictly forbidden by tradition.

As Giulio Gonfalonieri, the music critic, later remarked, everyone in the house must have been envious of Giuseppe di Stefano who sang Cavaradossi, for he could embrace Tosca—Renata Tebaldi.

Then the house fell silent and every auditor listened breathlessly to every note, every nuance of Renata's singing. There was not a single blemish in her performance, nothing that even the severest Callasiani could criticize. All of them felt they were hearing the best of Tebaldi, perhaps a more mature and sophisticated artist than before, but with the same perfection of phrasing and delivery. The famous words: "*E avanti a lui tremava tutta Roma,*" with which Tosca leaves Scarpia after she kills him, had perhaps even more profound effect than her singing of the aria "Vissi d'arte," for which she is known all over the world to be above any comparison. In a singularly cool but emphatic way she pronounced the phrase

191

evoking all the dreaded meaning of a people's terror before a tyrant.

The ovation after the performance will live in operatic annals as one of the greatest triumphs of any singer at La Scala. Thousands of carnations were rained on Tebaldi as she came forward countless times to take her bow. One would think that after such a triumph Renata would join her colleagues to celebrate her success. The proprietor of the Savini restaurant in the Galleria nearby invited the cast to a supper, but Renata excused herself. She went home where with her Aunt Marianna and Tina she had a quiet dinner. This was not the end but only the beginning of her engagement at La Scala—she had before her three more performances of *Tosca,* and four of *Andrea Chenier.* It was a highly emotional event for her and she wanted to remain quiet.

She must have felt fully satisfied with the reception the Milanese gave her, for she had already heard that the most militant Callasiani had joined in the applause and had at last declared peace. She was satisfied but not completely happy. She missed her mother. Giuseppina had been with her when she suffered agonies before she made her decision to leave La Scala. Mamma was the one who comforted her with her "Never mind, there will be a day, you'll be back." And now Mamma should have been at La Scala on the night of December 9.

Five weeks later, while Renata was completing her engagement at La Scala—she still had to give one more performance of *Andrea Chenier* before leaving for the United States—she received a telephone call from Langhirano.

"It was my cousin Tilde," Renata told me later. "Tilde said that she had had a letter from my father's sister-in-law informing her that he had suffered a hemorrhage in his nose and had to be taken to a hospital. The letter made it sound very grave. Naturally I immediately called my driver and with Marianna and Tina we drove to Guastalla where my father was in the hospital. It was very cold, a terrible day: it snowed and the roads were covered with ice. It took us almost three hours to cover a distance of one hundred and eighty kilometers, about a hundred miles.

"When we arrived I remained with Tina in the waiting room while Marianna went to see my father. I knew that his wife would be with him and I didn't want to meet her. After Marianna talked with him for a while and told him that I was waiting to see him, his wife left so I didn't have to see her.

"I went in. This was the first time we had met in eighteen years. We were both moved, but we never mentioned the past, not a word. My father spoke of my success, and how proud he was of me. Then they called in the reporters and the photographers. I have no idea how they all knew that I was there. It is a mystery to me." (Apparently Renata did not attribute any significance to her father's remark when he saw her: "I knew, I was

193

sure, that you would come as soon as you heard from Tilde.")

"Later, I saw him again before I left for New York," Renata continued.

"Did he have to have an operation?" I asked her.

"Oh no. It was not so grave as the letter made it out to be. But his doctor did tell me that his heart is not very good. After all, he is sixty-eight."

"And how does he feel now?"

"He is all right," Renata said. "He used to work in the city administration in Gualtieri, in Reggio Emilia, and working at the office, walking there and back home was too strenuous for him. But from now on he is not going to work any more."

"And now that you have seen him, how do you feel about him?" I asked.

"Not any differently than before. How could I?" Renata paused for a while and then added: "But I have a clear conscience. I have done my part." (Renata meant that she had settled an annuity on her father for the rest of his life.)

"So this closes the circle, doesn't it?" Renata said as she drew a ring in the air with her forefinger. "I am back at La Scala, and I have made peace with my father." The smile was gone from her face; she looked somber and pensive. I imagine she was thinking of her mother.

"And now what?" she asked, taking a deep breath that could have been a sigh.

194

"Now you mustn't sing too much. Am I the only one who has been telling you this for years?"

"Oh yes, I know. I have heard it so many times. But don't you remember me in Vienna, don't you remember how I felt when I was denied the opportunity to sing? I have told you then and I can only repeat it, I cannot live without it. And wait, I know exactly how and what you are going to say: you are going to point your finger at me and say 'You will ruin your voice.' Well, I may, and I may even lose it—only then I'll stop. But until then I shall sing as much as I can, for I love to sing and I cannot live without it."

How could anyone argue with her? I could not, for beside this, she once confessed to me that after a long interruption in her appearances on the stage she finds it difficult to get back into the swing of it. I have heard such complaints from a great many public performers and their anxiety about it is quite understandable. At present she is planning to sing all over the world as she has been doing for the past five years. She was invited to come to Russia, and there will be other people from other countries who will want to hear her. She will give the best Tebaldi performances, and yet there will be times when she will refuse to take an extra bow because she thinks she did not deserve it. There will be reviews written by music critics which will read like odes, where after exhausting the vocabulary of praise they will say that Renata Tebaldi sang as if she had invented the art

195

of singing, and there will be reviews in which a critic will not be satisfied with the sound of her middle, or her upper, or her lower register, and will say that a particular D flat was not quite on pitch. There will often be many in the audiences who will compare her to, and regret that she does not sing like, another singer who happens to be a coloratura. There will be some who lacking in any concrete observations will complain about Renata's costume, or her coiffure, or the way she moves her left arm when they would have preferred her to use her right. But all this will be of no consequence.

To a performing artist it is far more important to hear the frenzied clamor to repeat an aria, even when the audience knows well the opera house rules strictly forbid encoring anything during the performance. It will always be most gratifying to Renata to hear of people like the young man in San Francisco who wrote to a New York magazine: "I 'carried a spear' in *Aida* and *Otello* when she sang and it was the first time I have ever heard chorus, artists, and stagehands all stop and listen to a performer's artistry."

And I may add to this what I heard myself when once I was trying to get on a plane from Rome to Milan. All the seats were sold out except for two which had been reserved for a couple of tourists. I pleaded with the man at the office to let me have one of them in case the two tourists would be willing to take the next plane. "Why are you in such a hurry? One would think that you were going to miss a Tebaldi performance," he said. I told the man that as a matter of fact I was going to see Tebaldi. "Ah, that is a different matter," he said, and leaning across the counter, he added in a confidential tone, "You know, we love Tebaldi not only as a singer but as a person. In our days women like her are very rare."

And indeed this is the summit of a performing artist's success, for to him *Vox Populi—Vox Dei.*

*Operas and Other Works
Sung by
Renata Tebaldi*

Adriana Lecouvreur	(Cilèa)
Aida	(Verdi)
L'Amico Fritz	(Mascagni)
Andrea Chénier	(Giordano)
L'Assedio di Corinto	(Rossini)
La Bohème	(Puccini)
Cecilia	(Refice)
Eugene Onegin	(Tchaikovsky)
Falstaff	(Verdi)
La Fanciulla del West	(Puccini)
Faust	(Gounod)
Fedora	(Giordano)
Fernando Cortez	(Spontini)
Giovanna D'Arco	(Verdi)
Lohengrin	(Wagner)
Madama Butterfly	(Puccini)
I Maestri Cantori (Die Meistersinger)	(Wagner)
Mefistofele	(Boito)
Le Nozze di Figaro	(Mozart)
Olimpia	(Spontini)
Otello	(Verdi)
Simon Boccanegra	(Verdi)

Tannhäuser	(Wagner)
Tosca	(Puccini)
La Traviata	(Verdi)
Turandot	(Puccini)
La Wally	(Catalani)
Messa da Requiem	(Verdi)
Te Deum	(Verdi)
St. Matthew Passion	(Bach)
Requiem Mass	(Mozart)
Stabat Mater	(Rossini)

Discography
of Renata Tebaldi Recordings
issued in the United States

COMPILED BY

GEORGE JELLINEK

I. OPERAS (Complete & Highlights)

OPERAS	CASTS	CONDUCTORS	ORCHESTRAS	COMPLETE		HIGHLIGHTS	
				mono	stereo	mono	stereo
Boito, *Mefistofele*	Del Monaco, Siepi, Cavalli	Serafin	A.S.C.	(London) A 4339	OSA 1307	5519	25083
Giordano, *Andrea Chénier*	Del Monaco, Bastianini, Corena	Gavazzeni	A.S.C.	" A 4332	OSA 1303	5483	25076
Giordano, *Andrea Chénier*	Soler, Savarese, Ferrein	Basile	R.I.	(Cetra) 1244		50169	
Mascagni, *Cavalleria Rusticana*	Bjoerling, Bastianini, Corsi	Erede	M.M.F.	(RCA) LM 6059	LSC 6059	2243	
Puccini, *La Bohème*	Bergonzi, Bastianini, Siepi	Serafin	A.S.C.	(London) A 4236	OSA 1208	5562	25201
Puccini, *La Bohème*	Prandelli, Inghilleri, Arie	Erede	A.S.C.	" A 4209		5076	
Puccini, *La Fanciulla del West*	Del Monaco, MacNeil, Tozzi	Capuana	A.S.C.	" A 4338	OSA 1306	5556	25196
Puccini, *Madama Butterfly*	Bergonzi, Sordello, Cossotto	Serafin	A.S.C.	" A 4337	OSA 1314	5522	25084
Puccini, *Madama Butterfly*	Campora, Inghilleri, Rankin	Erede	A.S.C.	" A 4306		5077	
Puccini, *Manon Lescaut*	Del Monaco, Borriello, Corena	Molinari-Pradelli	A.S.C.	" A 4316	OSA 1317		
Puccini, *Tosca*	Del Monaco, London, Corena	Molinari-Pradelli	A.S.C.	" A 4235	OSA 1210	5584	25218
Puccini, *Tosca*	Campora, Mascherini, Corena	Erede	A.S.C.	" A 4213		5280	
Puccini, *Turandot*	Bjoerling, Nilsson, Tozzi	Leinsdorf	R.O.	(RCA) LM 6149	LSC 6149		

				(London)			
Puccini, *Turandot*	Del Monaco, Borkh, Zaccaria	Erede	A.S.C.	A 4320	OSA-1308	5553	25193
Verdi, *Aida*	Bergonzi, MacNeil, Simionato	Von Karajan	V.P.	" A 4345	OSA 1313	5568	25206
Verdi, *Aida*	Del Monaco, Protti, Stignani	Erede	A.S.C.	" A 4308		5279	
Verdi, *La Forza del Destino*	Del Monaco, Bastianini, Siepi	Molinari-Pradelli	A.S.C.	" A 4408	OSA 1405	5513	25085
Verdi, *Otello*	Del Monaco, Protti, Ribacchi, Corena	Erede	A.S.C.	" A 4312			
Verdi, *La Traviata*	Poggi, Protti, Di Palma	Molinari-Pradelli	A.S.C.	" A 4314		5344	
Verdi, *Il Trovatore*	Del Monaco, Savarese, Simionato	Erede	S.R.	" A 4326	OSA 1304	5521	25040

Orchestras:
A.S.C. Accademia di Santa Cecilia, Rome
R.I. Radio Italiana
M.M.F. Maggio Musicale Fiorentino
R.O. Rome Opera House
V.P. Vienna Philharmonic
S.R. La Suisse Romande

II. OPERATIC COLLECTIONS

RENATA TEBALDI
SINGS
Decca DL 4005
cond. Nino Sanzogno
(D)

Puccini, *La Bohème*, "Mi chiamano Mimi"

Puccini, *La Bohème*, "Donde lieta uscì"

Giordano, *Andrea Chénier*, "La mamma morta"

Catalani, *La Wally*, "Ebben, ne andrò lontana"

RENATA TEBALDI
OPERATIC RECITAL
London 5007
cond. Alberto Erede

Verdi, *Aida*, "Ritorna vincitor"

Gounod, *Faust*, "Le roi de Thule"

Gounod, *Faust*, "Air des bijoux"

Puccini, *Madama Butterfly*, "Un bel di vedremo"

Puccini, *Manon Lescaut*, "In quelle trine"

Puccini, *Tosca*, "Vissi d'arte"

Verdi, *Il Trovatore*, "Tacea la notte placida"

RENATA TEBALDI
OPERATIC RECITAL
No. 2
London 5174
(excerpts taken from complete sets 4209, 4306, 4316, 4308, 4312, 4314)
cond. Erede and
Molinari-Pradelli

Puccini, *La Bohème*, "Mi chiamano Mimi"

Puccini, *La Bohème*, "Donde lieta uscì"

Puccini, *Madama Butterfly*, "Tu, tu, piccolo Iddio"

Puccini, *Manon Lescaut*, "L'ora o Tirsi"

Puccini, *Manon Lescaut*, "Sola, perduta, abbandonata"

Verdi, *Aida*, "Pur ti riveggo; Ah no, fuggiamo!" (with Del Monaco)

206

OPERATIC COLLECTIONS (*Cont.*)

London 5174 (cont.)

Verdi, *La Traviata*, "Ah, fors'è lui"
Verdi, *La Traviata*, "Sempre libera"
Verdi, *La Traviata*, "Addio del passato"
Verdi, *Otello*, "Salce, Salce"
Verdi, *Otello*, "Ave Maria"

FAMOUS OPERATIC
DUETS
London 5175
(excerpts from complete sets
4308, 4312, 4316)
with Mario del Monaco,
tenor
cond. Erede and
Molinari-Pradelli

Verdi, *Aida*, Nile Scene (Act III)
Verdi, *Aida*, "La fatal pietra; O terra addio"
Verdi, *Otello*, "Già nella notte densa" (Act I)
Verdi, *Otello*, "Dio ti giocondi o sposo" (Act III)
Puccini, *Manon Lescaut*, "Tu, tu, amore" (Act II)

RENATA TEBALDI
OPERATIC RECITAL
No. 3
London 5202
(stereo) 25020
cond. Alberto Erede

Mozart, *Le Nozze di Figaro*, "Porgi amor"
Mozart, *Le Nozze di Figaro*, "Dove sono"
Cilea, *Adriana Lecouvreur*, "Io son l'umile ancella"
Cilea, *Adriana Lecouvreur*, "Poveri fiori"
Catalani, *La Wally*, "Ne mai dunque avrò pace"
Mascagni, *Lodoletta*, "Flammen, perdonami"
Rossini, *William Tell*, "Selva opaca"
Refice, *Cecilia*, "Per amor di Gesù"
Refice, *Cecilia*, "Morte di Cecilia"

OPERATIC COLLECTIONS *(Cont.)*

**RENATA TEBALDI
SINGS VERDI**
London 5520
(stereo) 25082
(excerpts from complete sets
4312, 4326, 4408)
cond. Alberto Erede and
Francesco Molinari-
Pradelli

Verdi, *Il Trovatore,* "Tacea la notte"
Verdi, *Il Trovatore,* "Di tal amor"
Verdi, *Il Trovatore,* "D'amor sull'ali"
Verdi, *Il Trovatore,* "Miserere; Tu
vedrai che amore" (Act IV)
Verdi, *La Forza del Destino,* "Me
pellegrina ed orfana"
Verdi, *La Forza del Destino,* "Ma-
dre pietosa vergine"
Verdi, *Otello,* "Salce, salce"
Verdi, *Otello,* "Ave Maria"

**RENATA TEBALDI
ITALIAN OPERA
ARIAS**
London 5561
(stereo) 25120
(excerpts from complete sets
4314, 4316, 4320, 4332, 4337,
4339, 4408)
cond. Erede, Serafin,
Gavazzeni, and Molinari-
Pradelli

Puccini, *Madama Butterfly,* "Un bel
di vedremo"
Puccini, *Madama Butterfly,* "Ancora
un passo"
Puccini, *Madama Butterfly,* "Con
onor muore"
Puccini, *Turandot,* "Signore ascolta"
Puccini, *Turandot,* "Tu che di gel"
Puccini, *Manon Lescaut,* "In quelle
trine morbide"
Puccini, *Manon Lescaut,* "Sola, per-
duta, abbandonata"
Verdi, *La Traviata,* "Addio del pas-
sato"
Verdi, *La Forza del Destino,* "Pace,
pace mio Dio"
Giordano, *Andrea Chénier,* "La
mamma morta"
Boito, *Mefistofele,* "L'altra notte"
Boito, *Mefistofele,* "Spunta l'aurora"

III. SONG RECITALS

RENATA TEBALDI
RECITAL
London 5267

RENATA TEBALDI
RECITAL
Vol. 2
London 5394

with Giorgio Favaretto, piano

with Giorgio Favaretto, piano

Anon., "Leggiadri occhi belli"
Scarlatti, "Le Violette"
Handel, "Piangerò la sorte mia"
Sarti, "Lungi dal caro bene"
Rossini, "La promessa"
Bellini, "Dolente imagine"
Bellini, "Vanne, o rosa fortunata"
Verdi, "Stornello"
Martucci, "Al folto bosco"
Martucci, "Cantava il ruscello"
Martucci, "Sul mar la navicella"
Favara, "A la barcillunisa"
Massetti, "Passo e non ti vedo"
Turina, "Cantares"

Scarlatti, "Chi vuole innamorarsi"
Scarlatti, "Caldo sangue"
Handel, "Ah, spietata"
Rossini, "La regata veneziana"
Mozart, "Ridente la calma," K. 152
Mozart, "Un moto di gioia," K. 579
Bellini, "Vaga luna che inargenti"
Bellini, "Per pietà bell'idol mio"
Mascagni, "M'ama, non m'ama"
Respighi, "Notte"
Tosti, " 'A vucchella"
Davico, "O luna che fa lume"

IV. INCIDENTAL APPEARANCES

Name of album	*Selection sung by Tebaldi*
LOVE DUETS FROM OPERAS Cetra 50178	Giordano, *Andrea Chénier* "Vicino a te; La nostra morte" duet with José Soler, tenor (from Cetra 1244)
EVENING AT THE LYRIC OPERA OF CHICAGO London 5320	Tchaikovsky, *Eugene Onegin* Tatiana's Letter Scene Boito, *Mefistofele* "L'altra notte" Ponchielli, *La Gioconda* "L'amo come il fulgor" (with Giulietta Simionato)
CESARE SIEPI OPERATIC RECITAL Vol. 2 London 5255	Verdi, *La forza del destino* Monastery Scene (with Siepi) Final trio (with Del Monaco and Siepi) (from A 4408)
JOHANN STRAUSS, *Die Fledermaus* GALA PERFORMANCE A 4347 London OSA 1319	Lehár, "Vilia-Lied"
OPERA EXCERPTS (Fill-in side for Barber's *Vanessa*) RCA Victor LM (LSC) 6138	Mascagni, *Cavalleria Rusticana* "Ah! lo vedi" (duet with Jussi Bjoerling) (from complete set LM 6059)

-- Index --

211

27-IV-69